Literacy in Action

Authors

Dr. Sharon Jeroski

Andrea Bishop
Jean Bowman
Lynn Bryan
Linda Charko
Maureen Dockendorf
Christine Finochio
Jo Ann Grime
Joanne Leblanc-Haley
Deidre McConnell
Carol Munro
Cathie Peters
Lorraine Prokopchuk
Arnold Toutant

PEARSON

Education
Canada

Grade 5 Project Team

Team Leader and Publisher: Anita Borovilos
National Literacy Consultants: Beth Ecclestone and Norma MacFarlane
Publishers: Susan Green and Elynor Kagan
Product Manager: Donna Neumann
Managing Editor: Monica Schwalbe
Developmental Editors: Amanjeet Chauhan, Elaine Gareau, Su Mei Ku, and Anne MacInnes
Production Editors: Amanjeet Chauhan and Adele Reynolds
Copy Editors: Lisa Santilli, Rebecca Vogan, and Jessica Westhead
Research: Nancy Belle Cook and Glen Herbert
Production Coordinators: Donna Brown and Zane Kaneps
Senior Manufacturing Coordinator: Jane Schell
Art Director: Zena Denchik
Designers: Zena Denchik, Maki Ikushima, Carolyn Sebestyen, Sonya V. Thursby/Opus House Inc., and Word & Image Design
Permissions Research: Cindy Howard
Photo Research: Nancy Belle Cook, Glen Herbert, Cindy Howard, and Terri Rothman
Vice-President Publishing and Marketing: Mark Cobham

ISBN-13: 978-0-13-201735-0 (softcover)
ISBN-10: 0-13-201735-0 (softcover)
ISBN-13: 978-0-13-204720-3 (hardcover)
ISBN-10: 0-13-204720-9 (hardcover)

Printed and bound in Canada.
1 2 3 4 5 TC 11 10 09 08 07

The publisher has taken every care to meet or exceed industry specifications for the manufacture of textbooks. The cover of this sewn book is a premium, polymer-reinforced material designed to provide long life and withstand rugged use. Mylar gloss lamination has been applied for further durability.

Acknowledgements

Series Consultants

Andrea Bishop
Anne Boyd
Christine Finochio
Don Jones
Joanne Leblanc-Haley
Jill Maar
Joanne Rowlandson
Carole Stickley

Specialist Reviewers

Science: Doug Herridge
  Toronto, ON
Social Studies: Marg Lysecki
  Toronto, ON
Aboriginal: Ken Ealey
  Edmonton, AB
Equity: Dianna Mezzarobba
  Vancouver, BC
Levelling: Susan Pleli
  Stoney Creek, ON
Iris Zammit
  Toronto, ON

Grades 3–6 Advisors and Reviewers

Dr. Frank Serafini
  Assistant Professor,
  University of Las Vegas,
  Las Vegas, Nevada

Patricia Adamson
  Winnipeg, MB
Marion Ahrens
  Richmond Hill, ON
Sandra Ball
  Surrey, BC
Gwen Bartnik
  Vancouver, BC
Jennifer Batycky
  Calgary, AB
Michelle Bellavia
  Hamilton, ON
Mary-Jane Black
  Hamilton, ON
Jackie Bradley
  Saskatoon, SK
Diane Campbell
  Durham, ON
Nancy Carl
  Coquitlam, BC
Janet Chow
  Burnaby, BC
Marla Ciccotelli
  London, ON
Susan Clarke
  Burlington, ON
Norma Collinson
  Truro, NS
Lynn Crews
  Lower Sackville, NS
Kathryn D'Angelo
  Richmond, BC

Susan Elliott
  Toronto, ON
Diane Gagley
  Calgary, AB
Michael Gallant
  Calgary, AB
Jennifer Gardner
  Vernon, BC
Adrienne Gear
  Vancouver, BC
Faye Gertz
  Niska, AB
Cindy Gordon
  Victoria, BC
James Gray
  Winnipeg, MB
Kathleen Gregory
  Victoria, BC
Myrtis Guy
  Torbay, NL
Kim Guyette-Carter
  Dartmouth, NS
Jackie Hall
  Vancouver, BC
Natalie Harnum
  Berwick, NS
Sherida Hassanali
  Herring Cove, NS
Deborah Holley
  Duncan, BC
Joanne Holme
  Surrey, BC
Patricia Horstead
  Maple Ridge, BC
Carol Hryniuk-Adamov
  Winnipeg, MB
Pamela Jacob
  Limestone, ON

Joanne Keller
  Delta, BC
Dawn Kesslering
  Regina, SK
Karen Quan King
  Toronto, ON
Linda Kirby
  Sault Ste. Marie, ON
Sheryl Koers
  Duncan, BC
Roger Lacey
  Calgary, AB
Sharon LeClair
  Coquitlam, BC
Caroline Lutyk
  Burlington, ON
Heather MacKay
  Richmond, BC
Margaret Marion
  Niagara Falls, ON
Sangeeta McAuley
  Toronto, ON
Paula McIntee
  Allanburg, ON
Caroline Mitchell
  Guelph, ON
Laura Mossey
  Durham, ON
Rhonda Nixon
  Edmonton, AB
Gillian Parsons
  Brantford, ON
Linda Perrin
  Saint John, NB
Charolette Player
  Edmonton, AB
Rhonda Rakimov
  Duncan, BC

Tammy Renyard
  Duncan, BC
Kristine Richards
  Windsor, ON
Kathryn Richmond
  St. Catharines, ON
Barbara Rushton
  New Minas, NS
Jaye Sawatsky
  Delta, BC
Michelle Sharratt
  Woodbridge, ON
Cathy Sheridan
  Ottawa, ON
Nanci-Jane Simpson
  Hamilton, ON
Kim Smith
  Newmarket, ON
Candace Spilsbury
  Duncan, BC
Sheila Staats
  Brantford, ON
Patricia Tapp
  Hamilton, ON
Vera Teschow
  Mississauga, ON
Joanne Traczuk
  Sutton West, ON
Sonja Willier
  Edmonton, AB
Susan Wilson
  St. Catharines, ON
Kelly Winney
  London, ON
Beth Zimmerman
  London, ON

CONTENTS

Independent Practice

Read! Write! Say! Do!

Your Literacy Portfolio

UNIT 5

It's a Mystery • 62

Read Together

Shared

Learn Together Poster

Guided Practice

What's the Mystery?

Literacy in Action

Independent Practice

Read! Write! Say! Do!

Your Literacy Portfolio

UNIT 6

We Are Canadian! •122

Independent Practice

Read! Write! Say! Do!

Your Literacy Portfolio

Get in the
Game

LEARNING GOALS

In this unit you will

- Read, view, and listen to opinions and information about games.

- Analyze the ideas writers and designers present.

- Present and support your own opinions, orally and in writing.

- Give and follow instructions for playing games.

learning new skills
challenging yourself
being competitive
negotiating
team spirit
having fun

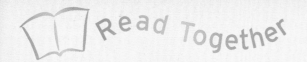
Ready, Set... Flop!

by Diana R. Jenkins
Illustrated by Ramón Pérez

Why is it important to try?

"Are you serious?"

Jacob looked me straight in the eye and said, "Jesse, I'm not joking."

"You're actually going out for track?"

He nodded—several times! "So, will you help me train?"

I rolled my eyes and said, "You know me—I am so *not* into team sports!"

"Then why do you always wear a baseball cap?" he demanded. "Why do you own three footballs and why do you have a basketball hoop over your—"

"So I'm a fan but I've never tried out for anything—not ever!" My attitude was always, '*Why bother?*' I wasn't good enough to make any team.

"Listen, Jake… ," I started—and stopped, because how do you tell the most uncoordinated guy in school that he doesn't stand a chance? "Listen, I… well… Well… all right. I'll help you."

"Great! So, meet at my house—after school— today!" he ordered.

So right after school was out, I dumped my books and hurried next door to find Jacob with his legs twisted around each other. And he was holding his right ear with his left hand!

"What the heck are you doing?" I asked.

"I'm stretching," he said, "and scratching." He
scratched his ear and promptly fell over.

I sighed as I helped him up onto his feet. "That's not
how you go about stretching!"

"I figured," he said, dusting himself off and grinning.
"So tell me—how do you go about it, Coach?"

This is hopeless! I thought. Aloud, I said, "Well, first
you need to warm up." I had Jacob walk briskly around
the block, and then I showed him the correct way to go
about stretching. Amazing—he only fell down twice!

"OK, now we'll need to work on distance running," I
said. "Run around the block four times."

Jacob took off, his arms and legs pumping. He couldn't
quite catch up with Mrs. Emerson and her ancient
poodle, but he came close. Then he turned the corner
and was out of sight.

I waited.

At last he returned, his arms flapping loosely, his mouth opening and closing like a baby bird's beak. He collapsed onto the grass, clutching his chest. Finally, he sat up. "Well, that's one down. Three to go!" he declared. He got up and ran down the block.

Each lap was slower than the previous one. Each time, Jacob collapsed, but he always struggled onto his feet again. When he staggered off for the fourth lap, I followed him. "Maybe that's enough for today," I suggested.

He grinned at me. "What kind of coach are you? You can't let me quit now!" He wobbled off.

Let him quit! How could I stop him?

The next afternoon I told Jacob that he needed to practise sprints.

"OK," he said. "What are sprints?"

"Fast, short runs," I explained. "For instance, a run from your driveway to the stop sign." *Maybe he can handle that*, I thought.

I was wrong. Although Jacob's legs worked like crazy, it took what seemed like a year for him to reach the stop sign. I could have *crawled* there and beaten him!

"How was that, Jesse?" he gasped, looking hopeful.

I handed him the water bottle. "I hate to have to tell you this, Jacob, but you're not much of a sprinter. Actually … to be honest… you're pretty hopeless."

"Yeah," he replied. He took a big swig of water.

Yes! I thought. *Finally he—*

"Actually, I think I'm more of a long-distance guy," he said. "So I guess I had better start practising my laps—eh, Coach?" He thrust the water bottle at me and took off around the block.

He was already tired, so the four laps took an eternity! My dad called me in for supper just as Jacob started his last lap. "Don't worry!" Jacob called. "I'll finish."

As if I didn't know that!

He trained for three weeks, and every day I wanted to tell Jacob that he was wasting his time, but somehow I couldn't say anything when I saw him working so hard.

Finally, it was the day before tryouts. "Are you going to watch?" Jacob asked.

I didn't want to see him flop (all that work and sweat for nothing!) so I said, "No. I don't want anybody to think I'm trying out."

"You *could* try out, you know," said Jacob. "You haven't been training like I have, but you just might make it."

"What?" I thought to myself, "Does this guy think he's a Superjock!"

"I would have a better chance than you do!" I snapped. "I don't even know why you're bothering!"

Jacob just stood there and looked at me for a minute before he said quietly, "At least I try." Then he walked away.

It turned out I was right because Jacob didn't make the team. But you know I wasn't happy to be right. All I could think about was how hard Jacob had kept trying and trying—and I'd never even tried at all.

So when I saw Jacob turning away from the sports bulletin board, I went over to him and said, "Hey, did you see the announcement about baseball tryouts?"

"Yeah," he said. "So?"

I swallowed. "I'm trying out. Do you want to train with me?"

He paused, and then smiled. "OK," he said and immediately barked, "My house! After school! Today!"

"I'll be there," I told him.

LET'S TALK ABOUT IT...

- How are games important in the boys' friendship?

- Explain why you agree or disagree that trying is important, even if you don't succeed.

Read Opinions

People have opinions about a lot of things! Some people write their opinions in newspapers or magazines. Other people give their opinions on Web sites or on television.

TALK ABOUT IT!

Think of an opinion article, editorial, or a review that you've read or seen.

- What was it about?
- What was the writer's or speaker's opinion?
- What were the main points? Did you agree?

Here are some places you can find opinions.

With a partner or group, make a list of people whose opinions you like to read or listen to.

People with Interesting Opinions

Cassie Campbell (athlete)

Raj Singh (my older brother)

Think Like a Reader

Read with a purpose

- Why do you read opinions?

Crack the code

- Writers often use specialized language when they write about an issue or activity. What strategies can help you understand the words?

Traditional Games
bluffing
negotiating

Make meaning

Practise using these strategies when you read opinions:

USE WHAT YOU KNOW	Before you read, look at the title and pictures to identify the topic. Then ask yourself: What do I already know about this topic?
VISUALIZE	Use the details to imagine the event or situation.
SYNTHESIZE	Put ideas together. How do the information and opinions compare with what you already know or believe?

Analyze what you read

- Think about who is writing or speaking. What do they want you to think or do? Why? Do you agree with them?
- Who might disagree? What might they say about the same topic?

HAVE YOUR SAY!

Traditional Games: Fun **and** Important

BY STUDENTS AT
NISGA'A ELEMENTARY
SCHOOL

**USE WHAT
YOU KNOW**

What do you know
about First Nations
games?

Nisga'a students demonstrate
how to play *Lahaal*, a guessing
game where players try to
trick each other.

We are from the Nisga'a nation and live in the Nass Valley in northern BC. Members of our class love to play video and computer games. We like to play basketball and soccer at school. When we hang out with our friends, we play ball tag. We also think it is very important to play the traditional games we learn from our Nisga'a teacher and our family members.

One traditional game we learned is called *Lahaal*. It is a team game that involves focusing, observing, bluffing, and negotiating. This game teaches skills that helped us to survive in the past, and those skills are still important today.

When we play *Lahaal*, we practise observing and staying focused. We observe other team members and remember the steps they have taken. Our ancestors needed to focus to be successful hunters and find food for their families. Observing helped our ancestors know the environment, respect nature, and notice changes that would affect our whole nation.

Another skill we use in *Lahaal* is bluffing to distract the other team. This makes it harder for them to remember what we have done.

Lahaal also teaches us to negotiate with the other team. Our ancestors negotiated so they could get what they needed to survive, such as smoked fish, crabs, moose meat, or oolichan grease, which is a kind of fish oil. Negotiating is an important skill we use when we trade with family members for things that we need.

In the time before European contact, the Nisga'a used many skills to hunt and harvest foods successfully for their families. Chiefs negotiated with other First Nations groups. For example, if someone crossed into traditional hunting and harvesting lands without permission, each chief would try to get the best deal for his nation.

Traditional games are an important part of our life. We learn to focus, have team spirit, negotiate with others, and have fun. Why not investigate a traditional game yourself?

VISUALIZE

Imagine playing these games long ago.

SYNTHESIZE

How are the skills people used in *Lahaal* like the skills in less traditional games?

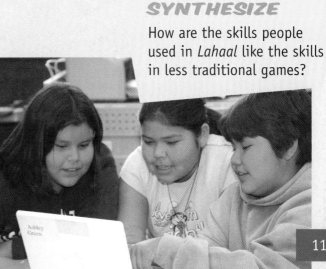

Students work on an opinion article.

11

HAVE YOUR SAY!

Internet Games: Fun **but** Be Aware!
BY STEFAN MOLGAT

USE WHAT YOU KNOW

What do you know about playing Internet games?

Stefan Molgat has some advice for his fellow Internet-game players.

Oh, this is fun! The weekend off and you are playing the Choco Chums Moon Game on the Choco Chums Chocolate Company Web site you heard about on TV. All of a sudden, an ad pops up. It says, *"Enter our contest and win a year's supply of candy."* Wow!

Now a new window pops up. It says, *"Type in your name, address, and telephone number here. Type your e-mail address here."* You are very excited. You type your name and address. That's one step closer. Now you type your telephone and e-mail. Almost done. You are about to click "send" ... S T O P!! Internet games can be fun but when you play them you need to be aware.

Most kids love to play Internet games. What kids may not know is that companies create Web sites and games just so they can advertise their products. These advertisers want to send messages about products that are just for kids. Can a 10-year-old be a match for the highly paid people behind these ad schemes? No way.

Kids need to pay attention to what is happening when they play games online. Contests are fun, but advertisers can use them to get personal information about kids. This can be dangerous, because the company that gets the information can use it in several ways. The company knows where to reach you. Your name is public property and can be sold to other companies who want you on their mailing list. You are under constant pressure to buy, buy, buy! This causes conflict with your parents—and it can empty your bank account if you keep buying things. Worse yet, you might get addicted to buying things off the Net.

VISUALIZE

Think about how you feel when you are playing an exciting Internet game.

Stefan at his computer

So, be informed. When you play on the Internet, stop and ask yourself:

- Am I being lured into buying products?
- Am I asked to give personal information?

If the answer is yes, stay away. Play for fun and be aware.

SYNTHESIZE

How are Internet games like electronic games? How are they different?

HAVE YOUR SAY!

Team Sports: Go for It!

BY NELLY CEPHAS

Nelly Cephas feels that playing team sports can teach you many things, such as respecting one another.

USE WHAT YOU KNOW

What do you know about team sports?

14

Team sports are one of the most important activities we can participate in during our lives. Some of you will say, "Team sports are dumb and boring." I disagree. Team sports can be fun. They also keep you fit and teach you about getting along with others.

Playing a team sport is a great way to get regular exercise. Exercising helps you build strong muscles and bones. Exercising also improves your coordination. In football, when you run and catch the ball at the same time, you are improving your coordination.

Playing on a team is an easy way to learn a new sport. You don't have to learn all by yourself. Together, you learn the rules and the strategies of the game. You learn by watching what some team members already know.

Being on a team helps you understand how important it is to get along with others. On a team, everyone needs to take turns so that no one feels left out. You learn how important it is to respect one another and be polite. And you learn to handle disappointment. It's hard to accept when your team loses, but you see that everyone on the team feels the same way and you support one another. Winning is a great feeling but losing can help you learn. You have to think about how you could have played better and then work on practising to do that in the next game.

VISUALIZE

How does it feel to be part of a team?

Nelly plays with a friend at school.

If you don't already play a team sport, think about joining one. You can count on improving your coordination, staying healthy, and feeling good about being part of a team. Try it! You will make new friends and have a lot of fun!

SYNTHESIZE

How are team sports like other games? How are they different?

15

Reflect on Your Reading

You have . . .

- talked about games.
- read other students' opinions about games.
- used strategies to read challenging words.

observing

bluffing

negotiating

strategies

coordination

traditional

I like to play team games. I like working together. It's more fun to celebrate with a team!

USE WHAT YOU KNOW

VISUALIZE

SYNTHESIZE

You have also . . .

- explored different reading strategies.

Write About Learning

How does thinking about what you know help you before you read? Use thinking bubbles to show what you did before reading the selections for "What's Your Opinion?" How did it help?

Read Like a Writer

When you write opinion articles, editorials, or letters, you want to make your readers *think* about your ideas. You want to be convincing!

TALK ABOUT IT!

- What do you notice about the way opinion articles are written?
- How are they different from information articles?
- What do you notice about the ideas?

Make a chart listing what you notice about the **ideas** in opinion writing.

HINT!

Look at how **details** and **examples** support the main ideas.

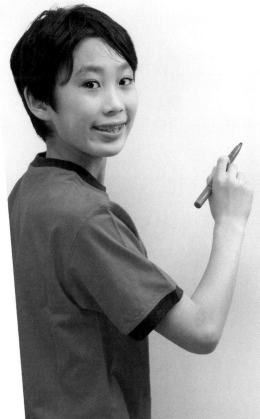

Ideas in Opinion Writing
- the main opinion is at the beginning
- there are convincing details and examples
- sounds like the writer knows a lot about the topic
- sometimes ends by telling the reader what to think or do

When Children Play,

Children at play in Uganda

Should all children have the right to play?

Who We Are

We are a charity called Right To Play. We use sport and play to help children and youth in countries where there can be hardships such as disease, bad weather, natural disasters, and war.

RIGHT TOPLAY

What We Do

Right To Play programs encourage the growth of children in many ways. Children become healthier through physical, social, and emotional growth. Our programs help to build safer and stronger communities. We insist that all children be included:

- children who are refugees;
- children who have been soldiers;
- children with physical or developmental challenges; and
- children who have been affected by HIV/AIDS or war.

Key Goals of Right To Play

Create Healthier, Educated Children

Sport and play programs guide children on a path to healthy development. The programs teach important values and life skills, but also spread joy and fun!

Plan for the Future

Right To Play trains local young people to be coaches, leaders, and role models. These young members can then help their communities to plan for the future. Programs will continue to run as leaders pass on their skills to the next generation.

READ LIKE A WRITER

How does the writer use examples of real people to make a convincing opinion?

"SINCE I WAS A CHILD, SPORT HAS BEEN A POWERFUL, POSITIVE FORCE IN MY LIFE. I BELIEVE EVERY CHILD HAS THE RIGHT TO PLAY."

– Dikembe Mutombo, Right To Play Athlete Ambassador and NBA basketball star (originally from Republic of Congo)

19

Build Safer, More Peaceful Communities

Right To Play programs teach how to prevent and resolve conflict. They teach respect for others, and fair play. We help to open up communication and understanding between groups who live in the same place.

Encourage Healthier Lifestyles

Sports festivals and sports heroes attract the attention of the young people in communities. Once we have their attention, we help make them aware of important health issues.

Right To Play Local Coach Profile

TAHMINA KHAN

Coach: Tahmina Khan
Location: Quetta, Pakistan

Tahmina's Story

Tahmina was born in Kabul, Afghanistan. When her father lost his job, Tahmina's family moved to Pakistan in 1990. Tahmina is now 17. Since 2004, Tahmina has been working with Right To Play as a coach.

Community Impact

Tahmina works with Afghan refugee children. She uses sport and play to help girls do more things by themselves. Tahmina's hard work has made a difference in her whole community. Now the girls are stronger and more confident. The community has more positive attitudes toward girls and women.

Look After Yourself, Look After One Another

Right To Play uses the Red Ball as our symbol. We play with this ball in our games. It is our teaching tool and our gift wherever we take our programs. The Red Ball goes to every school, every community, and every refugee camp.

Our motto is written on the ball in different languages. It says, "Look After Yourself, Look After One Another." This motto guides everything we do. We stress the best qualities and skills that sport and play can bring. These are:

- a positive view
- respect and kindness toward others
- courage
- leadership
- inspiration
- joy

CATRIONA LE MAY DOAN

"I BELIEVE IN THE POWER OF SPORT AND PLAY TO CHANGE LIVES."

– Catriona Le May Doan, Right To Play Athlete Ambassador and two-time Canadian Olympic Gold Medallist

Right To Play's Red Ball is used in a game in Pakistan.

PUBLISHED: MONDAY, FEBRUARY 27, 2006

For All the Right Reasons

MICHAEL PETRIE,
Calgary Herald

Clara Hughes skated 5000 m in six minutes and 59.07 seconds to win an Olympic gold medal.

TURIN, ITALY – Clara Hughes skated 5000 metres at an indoor rink Saturday night in Turin and the world became a better place.

...In six minutes and 59.07 seconds, Hughes earned Olympic gold.

Then she took a seat behind the microphone and showed what truly makes her a champion.

"I was alone in the room this morning, passing time," said the 33-year-old from Winnipeg. She lives and trains in Calgary. "I turned on the TV and saw a documentary about Right To Play.

"I'd been thinking all week about the meaning of sport and what motivates me, and why I love to compete.

"When I saw those kids, I think they were in Uganda, they were smiling and I thought, that's what it's all about. Play can give so much to the world, so much hope, so much positive energy."

MEDIA WATCH

Look online and in other media for stories of other athletes who are involved in Right To Play. What are their reasons for supporting it?

DIG DEEPER

1. Make a list of reasons why people support Right To Play. Put a star beside the two reasons that are most important to you.

2. With a partner or group, make up a poem, song, or rap convincing people to support Right To Play.

Are We There Yet?
A Map Sport

by Ira Rosofsky

What kind of game can you play with a map?

Want a workout for your body while you use your brain? Try orienteering. This is a race across unknown **terrain** where you use only a map and a compass. It's quite easy to learn, but presents many challenges. And since the equipment is just a map and a compass, it's a sport almost everyone can take part in.

The history of the sport goes back to the end of the 19th century. Swedish soldiers created the term "orienteering." It means to cross a new territory using a map and compass. Today, thousands of people in North America take part in orienteering events.

terrain (te-RAIN)
an area of land

READ LIKE A WRITER
How does the writer make the ideas clear?

23

This girl stops to orient her map. To do this, she sets it according to the compass. She can then get to the next control point on a course.

topographic
(TO-po-GRAPH-ic)
showing features of the land such as hills, fences, and streams

What's It Like?

People who take part in the sport are called orienteers. They usually use **topographic** maps that show landmarks such as trails, streams, and fences. In most events, orienteers use maps that also show a series of checkpoints called control points. On the course itself, these map points are locations with flag markers. You use your compass and your knowledge of maps to visit various control points in a certain order. The first one to visit all the control points wins.

The sport can involve walking, running, biking, skiing, or even canoeing. Orienteers get to travel to all kinds of outdoor locations.

Even toddlers can take part in an orienteering string-course event. The little kids follow strings that connect from one control point to the next. Older kids and beginners of any age might try a White course. These courses are usually about 1.5 to 5 kilometres long, and all the control points are located at major land features. The next step after White is Yellow. These courses are still easy, but the control point might be off the trail rather than right on it. It becomes harder as orienteers progress to the expert courses—Green, Red, and Blue.

Orienteers often use topographic maps like this one that show details of the landscape.

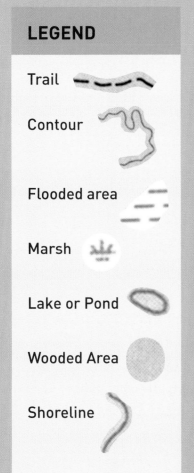

LEGEND

Trail

Contour

Flooded area

Marsh

Lake or Pond

Wooded Area

Shoreline

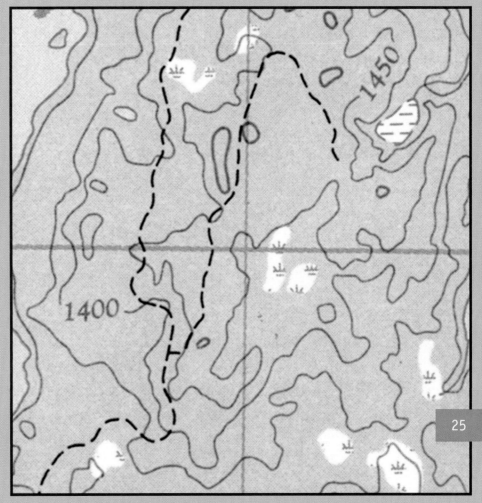

1450

1400

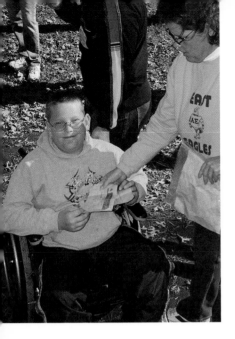

Orienteers getting ready for an event. Courses can be set up to combine different levels of skill and speed.

Expert courses are longer and the terrain is more difficult. Expert orienteers travel through deep woods. They must depend on their compasses because they can't see very far ahead.

Orienteering also has events for people with physical challenges. Wheelchair events combine easy travel over trails with difficult placements of control markers. Speed is less important when you have to use your map and compass to pick out the correct control marker from a group of wrong ones.

Navigation is the key skill for the orienteer. You start by knowing where you are on a map. You place your compass on the known map location. Next, you calculate the direction to the first control point—north, for example. Then you hold up your compass and use it to orient you to the north. And off you go. It sounds simple, but how easy can it be if you can't see any farther ahead than the tree in front of you? If you like a challenge, try orienteering!

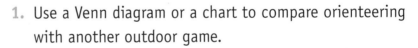

DIG DEEPER

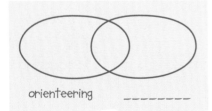

orienteering _ _ _ _ _ _ _ _

1. Use a Venn diagram or a chart to compare orienteering with another outdoor game.

2. In a group, create an orienteering course in your school or on your school grounds with five control points. Give your map to another group and challenge them to complete your course. After you complete the course, meet with your group to decide whether you think orienteering is an interesting sport.

The Wacky Games
Hall of Fame

READ LIKE A WRITER
How do writers use words that sound the same to create jokes?

Q Why did the golfer need new socks?

A Because he had a hole in one!

Q Why was the spider the best outfielder on the team?
A Because he caught lots of flies.

Watch Out for Those Dice!

This Monopoly® board in California is a square with each side 9 m long. Participants play with jumbo dice and wear gigantic token-shaped hats.

27

What might you find in a Wacky Games Hall of Fame?

Kylie: After the cycling race, my bike wouldn't even stand up.

Emma: Why not?

Kylie: It was two-tired!

Amit: I've been skating since I was 6 years old.

Lin: Wow, you must be **really tired.**

Q Why is it a bad idea to tell jokes while playing hockey?

A The ice might *crack up!*

An A-"maze"-ing Race

Neil Switzer created this maze near Smithville, Ontario. It has more than 3 km of confusing paths, many leading nowhere. Can you see the beaver sitting on a log with the maple leaf?

Record-Toppling Feat

Ma Lihua of China sits beside the dominoes she's just toppled to set a world record. The 4-km long line of dominoes took her seven weeks to set up, but just four minutes to knock down.

Q How is an airplane pilot like a football player?

A They both want to make safe touchdowns.

Nick: Where do you keep your baseball mitt?

Anya: In the glove compartment!

Check Mate!

In Argentina, human chess pieces replay a famous chess game.

How Many Points for Lifting This Letter?

Two teams in England play a game of Scrabble® on a square board with each side 30 m long. Each tile is a square that has sides 2 m long.

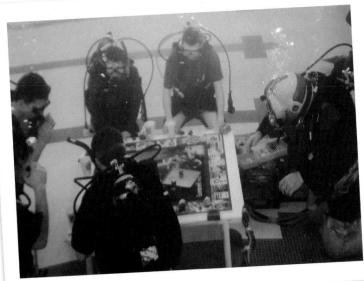

May I Buy Water Works?

The game pieces in this game of underwater Monopoly® are specially weighted so they won't float away.

Q Why was the soccer stadium always cool?

A Because it had a fan in every seat!

DIG DEEPER

1. Collect or create other jokes or weird facts about games.

2. Make up a game or a record that could be in the Wacky Games Hall of Fame. Write a convincing argument telling why it should be included.

Just Play the Game

Words from Words

Here's What You Need

- 2 players
- 2 pencils
- a few sheets of paper
- dictionary
- egg timer or stopwatch

READ LIKE A WRITER

How does the writer use specific examples to make the instructions easy to understand?

Here's What You Do

Object of the game: To make the greatest number of words in the shortest amount of time.

1. Both players think up a word, preferably a long one, to use for the game. Here is an example: *pronunciation*.

2. Each player takes a pencil and a sheet of paper. Both players print the one word they chose at the top of their paper.

3. When both players are ready, one player starts the timer, and the game begins. Each player must come up with as many words as possible in two minutes, using only letters from the chosen word. Here are some words you can make from *pronunciation*: pro, tin, noun, rot, action.

4. Each player checks the other's list, using the dictionary if necessary. The player with the most correct words wins.

What games can you play without any special equipment?

Inupiat Maq

Here's What You Need

- 3 or more players

Here's What You Do

Object of the game: To make the other players laugh.

1. Gather everyone together and sit in a circle. One player is selected to begin the game.

2. The person selected must make the other players laugh by making faces or using body movements, but is not allowed to make any noises. Whoever laughs first takes the next turn at trying to make the others laugh. You can continue playing until everyone has had a turn.

DIG DEEPER

1. Try both games. Which one did you like best? Why? Write a short review, giving and supporting your opinion.

2. Research to find another game from around the world that would be easy to play in your classroom. Teach it to your group.

Season's Tickets

by Jean Little
Illustrated by Ramón Pérez

READ LIKE A WRITER
What details does the poet include to make the events seem real?

My big sister Barbara is bats about baseball.
When my father gave me *Touching All the Bases*
By Claire Mackay as a present,
I read bits of it.
It was pretty good.
It made me laugh.
But Barbara memorized it.
Just ask her.
She knows every single baseball fact in that book
And lots Claire Mackay didn't put in.

33

What makes someone care about a game?

Yet when Dad got two season's tickets to the Dome,
He meant me to go with him.
Taking Barbara never crossed his mind.

Well, baseball's okay,
But I don't want to waste all my summer weekends
Watching the Jays
Run around on those miles of Astroturf.

I want to be a scientist.
I want to learn all I can
About turtles and toads and snakes.
I like reading books about them, but
I want to observe them too.
I like being outside in swamps or beside creeks.
I lie on my stomach and watch them for hours.
I don't care how many mosquitoes bite me.

I tried to tell Dad, but he refused to listen.

Barbara's twelfth birthday is on May 22.

I bought a card.
"This card entitles you to take my place
At all the baseball games
Dad is going to this summer," I wrote.
"Happy birthday."

Dad was miffed.
He hardly spoke to me for about a week.
But the first time he took Barbara,
They had such a great time
That I don't think he'll want to take me ever again.

She knows everybody's batting average,
Which team they used to play for,
What pitches they shouldn't try.

Before they are out of the driveway,
Mom smiles at me and picks up her book.
I smile back and head for the nearest toad terrain.

It was the best present I ever gave anybody.
The cheapest too.

DIG DEEPER ··

1. Who is telling the story in this poem, a brother or a sister?
   How do you know? List at least three other things you know
   about the speaker and give evidence from the poem.

2. In a group of three, role-play one of the situations in the
   poem. Then write a journal entry telling about your own part.

Team Spirit

What does a logo say about a team?

SAINT JOHN
SEA DOGS

SIX NATIONS
ARROWS
EXPRESS

SLEDGE DOGS

NAIT
OOKS

MEDIA WATCH

Look for interesting team logos when watching sports on TV. Where are they displayed?

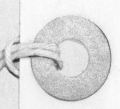

DIG DEEPER

1. Make a 2-column table. In the first column, tell the main object/animal the logo shows. In the second column, give one or two words describing the impression the logo gives.

2. Design your own logo for a sports team. Think about the idea you want to send. Choose the image and colours that best represent your idea.

Opinion Writers at Work!

You have read other people's opinions about games. Now it's your turn to write an opinion article for other students to read.

Choose Your Topic

- With a group, brainstorm a list of opinion topics.
- You might write a review telling your opinion of a video or Internet game.
- You might write about why students should or should not play a particular kind of game.
- You might write about why winning is or is not important.

Write Your Opinion Article

- Think about your purpose. What do you want your readers to think or do?
- Start by stating your opinion clearly.
- Make a list of reasons and evidence. Choose the most convincing ones.
- End by telling your readers what you want them to think or do.
- Work with an editing partner to improve your article.

TIPS FOR TOPICS

- Write about something you care about.
- Think about your audience—what would other students like to read about?
- Look at topics in this unit or in magazines you like.

Publish Your Opinion Article

- Use a computer to produce your final copy.
- Proofread carefully!
- Create a catchy headline and include a photograph or illustration.
- Add your article to the class collection for your classmates to read.
- Think about publishing it on the Web!

THINK ABOUT POINT OF VIEW

To develop strong arguments, think about the arguments someone who disagreed with you might make. How could you answer their arguments?

Video Games May Help Relieve Pain

by Catherine Clarke Fox

Patients who play handheld video games seem to be less worried while waiting in a hospital.

How can video games be good for you?

A lot of grown-ups worry that spending too much time playing video games isn't good for a kid's health. But some doctors have noticed that kids who bring their handheld game players to the hospital seem less worried about being there. These patients also seem to experience less pain when they are concentrating on a superhero adventure or a car race.

At the Johns Hopkins Children's Center in Baltimore, Maryland, young patients are finding hospital visits easier to deal with. This is thanks to a test program called the Hospital-based Online Pediatric Environment (HOPE).

Dr. Arun Mathews looks on as a patient plays a virtual race car game.

Patients in HOPE have a life-threatening kidney condition. Their kidneys can no longer filter wastes from their blood. To get their blood cleaned, these kids must be hooked up to dialysis (dye-AL-uh-sis) machines at the hospital. They need to have this procedure three times a week and each session lasts at least three hours. HOPE allows kids to play online sports, racing, and adventure games with each other. Eventually they will be able to connect with kids in other hospitals who are undergoing the same procedure.

"These kids often feel isolated by their illness. We want to use the power of the Internet to bring kids together. This program would let them know they are not alone," said Arun Mathews, the doctor who heads the program. He loves video games himself and thought up the idea to connect kids all over the country through those games.

READ LIKE A WRITER
How does the writer use specific examples to make the information easy to understand?

43

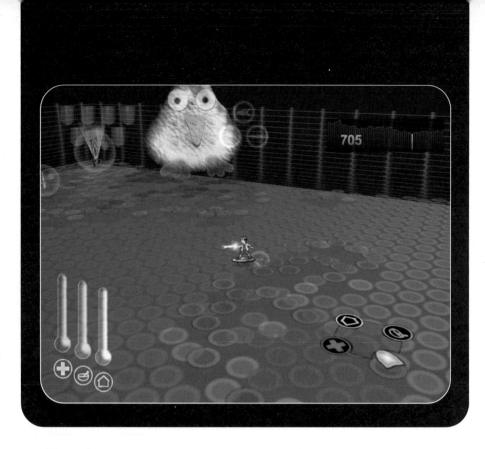

Elsewhere, many researchers are testing video programs that might help young patients. For example, nine-year-old Ben Duskin was struggling with cancer. He helped to design the video game (pictured above) in which players get rid of cancer cells.

That's all great news, because doctors already know that reducing pain and worry helps patients heal faster.

DIG DEEPER

1. Use a 5-W chart (who, what, when, where, why) to summarize the information in this Internet article.

2. Make up a slogan for the HOPE project. Draw a picture of a T-shirt with the slogan.

5 W's	information
who	
what	
where	
when	
why	

Young patients are not the only ones who get to be heroes in the virtual world of HOPE! Here are some of the identities taken on by doctors and other hospital workers involved in the game.

Real Name:
Dr. Arun Mathews
HOPE Alias:
DiscoSanchez

Real Name:
Mary White
HOPE Alias:
BlueStreak

Real Name:
Robert Swain
HOPE Alias:
Infonaut

Real Name:
Dr. David DeMaso
HOPE Alias:
LanceSpectacular

Real Name:
Dr. Sue Furth
HOPE Alias:
UltraViolet

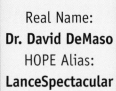

Real Name:
Dr. Harold Lehmann
HOPE Alias: **StarFox**

Fox Trot

by Bill Amend

MEDIA WATCH

Collect comic strips and cartoons that show different games. What ideas about games do they emphasize?

DIG DEEPER

1. Design a cover for a new video game that is based on a real game people play.

2. Compare video games and active games.

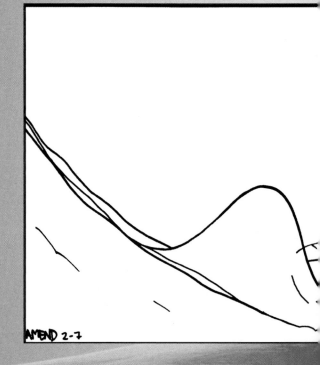

AMEND 2-7

Can you learn a real game by playing a video game?

HOOPS

Robert Burleigh

ILLUSTRATED BY

Stephen T. Johnson

Hoops.
The game.
Feel it.
The rough roundness.
The ball
like a piece
of the thin long reach
of your body.
The way it answers whenever you call.
The never-stop back and forth flow,
like tides going in, going out.
The smooth,
skaterly glide
and sudden swerve.
The sideways slip
through a moment of narrow space.
The cool.
The into
and under
and up.
The feathery fingertip roll
and soft slow drop.
Feel your throat on fire.
Feel the asphalt burning beneath your shoes.
The two-of-you rhythm.
The know-where-everyone-is without having to look.
The watching
and waiting
to poke
and pounce.
The fox on the lurk.
The hunger.
The leap from the pack.

How do you
feel when you're
doing something
you love?

READ LIKE A WRITER
How does the poet use
sensory details to help the
reader visualize the game?

49

The out-in-the-clear
like a stallion
with wind in your face.
The bent legs tense
as the missed shot swirls
and silently spins.
The hawk.
Your arm shooting up
through a thicket of arms.
The lean
and brush
and burst free.
The skittery,
cat-footed dance
along the baseline.
The taste
for the rock in your hands
when it counts the most.

The weight of you
hanging from fine,
invisible threads.
The eyes.
The arc.
The no-sound
sound of the ball
as it sinks
through nothing but still,
pure air.
Yes.
Hoops.
The game.
Feel it.

DIG DEEPER

1. With a group, perform this poem as a choral reading. Consider
   having some group members act out parts of the poem as you read.

2. Write a poem about a favourite activity. Use sensory words to
   show how it makes you feel. Look at "Hoops" for ideas.

The First Olympic Games

Retold by Jean Richards
Illustrated by Kat Thacker

Once upon a time, long ago in ancient Greece, there lived a man whose name was Tantalus. He was half man and half god, because his father was the great Greek god Zeus.
Tantalus had a son, Pelops. He had treated his son horribly, but the gods felt sorry for Pelops and gave him many presents. The best present of all was a chariot with a team of snow-white horses that could run faster than the wind.

53

How might the Olympic Games have started?

"Take these horses," said Zeus to Pelops, "and find yourself a kingdom, for you shall become a great ruler."

Pelops thanked the gods and, waving good-bye to them, he mounted his chariot and galloped down the dusty mountain road and out onto the plain.

As he came around a curve he reined in his horses, for he saw an old man dressed in rags by the side of the road.

"Where are you going?" shouted the old man.

"I'm off to find a kingdom," Pelops replied.

"I have an idea for you," said the old man. "I know of a kingdom called Elis, where a beautiful princess lives. Her name is Hippodamia. The man who marries the princess will inherit her father's kingdom."

"That sounds perfect," said Pelops.

"There's just one problem," cautioned the old man. "If you want to marry the princess you have to run a chariot race against the old king. If you win, you get the princess and the kingdom. If you lose, you get your head chopped off. So far, twelve people have lost."

"I won't lose," said Pelops. "My horses can run faster than the wind."

"But the king's can run faster than lightning," warned the old man.

"I am not afraid," said Pelops. He thanked the old man and started off.

"Remember," the old man called after him, "when you see a palace gate with twelve heads stuck on it, you'll know you're at the right place."

Pelops's horses practically flew along the road. After many hours they came to the gate with the twelve heads. Pelops got down from his chariot and asked to see the king.

READ LIKE A WRITER
How does the writer make events in the story seem real?

The servants led him through a magnificent garden full
of green figs and crimson pomegranates to the huge throne
room. There, on a golden throne, sat the king. Next to him
stood the beautiful princess, Hippodamia. Her black eyes
sparkled like stars when she saw the handsome young
visitor.

Pelops bowed low before the king. "I have come to
woo your daughter," he said.

The king invited Pelops to share a sumptuous dinner
of meats, breads, and wines served in bowls made of
hammered gold and silver. "My daughter and my kingdom
are yours," he said, "if you win the chariot race."

"My horses can run faster than the wind," said Pelops.

"Mine can run faster than lightning," countered the king.

"My horses were given to me by the great god Zeus," boasted Pelops.

The king said nothing. He had never lost a race. His horses were magic and had been given to him by Ares, the god of war.

"Tomorrow morning at sunrise," the king declared, "the race shall begin."

Later that evening, the princess wandered out near the king's stables. She did not see the stable boy, who was brushing the horses' shiny black coats so they would look their best for the race in the morning. Hippodamia looked up at the starlit sky and said to herself, dreamily, Oh, I do wish my father would lose the race, just this once.

Now the stable boy, who had always adored the princess from afar, overheard Hippodamia. I can make her wish come true, he thought. He did not tell the princess of his plan.

After the princess went inside, he carefully took out the bronze pins that held the great wooden wheels on the chariot and replaced them with pins made of candle wax.

The next morning, as the orange sun peeped over the mountaintops, the royal musicians sounded their horns. Crowds of people gathered on the lush green fields of Olympia.

The king stood in his chariot, his helmet gleaming in the sun. He was hardly able to hold back his snorting horses.

Clouds of dust rose up around the galloping horses.

"On, my fiery steeds," shouted the king.

"Faster!" shouted Pelops.

The crowd cheered. The horses galloped neck and neck, faster than wind, faster than lightning.

Now, thought the king, I will pull ahead and win!

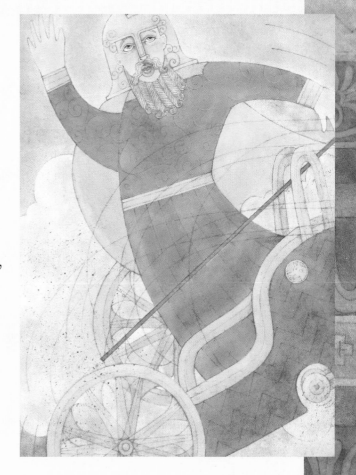

He whipped his horses harder, but instead of speeding up, they fell behind. Something was wrong! The wax pins had melted in the heat.

Suddenly the wheels flew off, and the king was thrown to his death.

Of course, Pelops had won the race, so he would marry Hippodamia and rule the kingdom. But Pelops and Hippodamia were very sad that the old king had died. He had not really been a mean king, you see. It's just that he had loved his daughter so much he didn't want to give her away in marriage.

So, before their wedding, Pelops and Hippodamia decided to have a great funeral feast in honour of the king.

They invited heroes from all over Greece to take part in athletic games and races, in remembrance of the king's great chariot race.

Pelops decreed that such games should be held every four years, till the end of time. And since the games took place on the fields of Olympia, they have been known ever since as the Olympic Games.

Pelops and his lovely Hippodamia went on to become wise and good rulers of the great kingdom of Elis.

True to Pelops's decree, the games were held every four years on the fields of Olympia. But around the year 500 there was a great earthquake that knocked down the buildings and a huge flood that covered the fields with water and mud. They remained buried for almost 1500 years. People forgot about the Olympic Games. Because no one could see the Olympic fields, many people believed the fields and the games had never even existed.

Imagine their surprise when, in 1875, archaeologists dug into the earth at just the right place and discovered the ancient fields of Olympia, where the games had taken place so long ago. There was great rejoicing around the world, and the Olympic Games were started once again.

And today the Olympic Games continue. Every four years, athletes from all over the world come together to compete in a spirit of peace and friendship.

The games are held in different countries, and an Olympic flame is always kept burning in the stadium until the games have ended.

This flame is lit from the rays of the sun on the Olympic fields in Greece.

The flame is carried by runners to the games, wherever they take place. It keeps alive that tiny spark from the great, red Mediterranean sun that shines down on the beautiful Olympic fields in Greece today, just as it did more than 2500 years ago.

DIG DEEPER

1. Make an illustrated story map to summarize this myth. Show the main characters, the setting, and at least four events.
2. With a partner, create a new myth or story about how the Olympic Games started. Tell your story orally to a small group.

Connect and Share

People enjoy learning and playing new games. It's your turn to teach one of the games you've learned!

Take a game home!

■ Choose a game you've learned to play at school. It might be one of the games in this unit.

■ Practise playing it to make sure you remember how.

■ Teach it to someone at home.

Bring a game back!

■ Ask your family members to teach you a game.

■ Choose a simple game that is easy to learn. It might be a puzzle, a word game, or a board game.

■ Practise it so you can teach it to a partner or group.

TIPS FOR TEACHING A GAME

● Gather any equipment you need.
● Explain the object of the game.
● Make a list of the important steps.
● Show each step clearly, one at a time.
● Use simple, clear language.

Spotlight on **Learning**

Collect

■ Gather your notebooks, your writing, and your projects from this unit.

Talk and reflect

Work with a partner.

■ Together, read the Learning Goals on page 2.

■ Talk about how well you met these goals.

■ Look over all your work for evidence.

Select

■ Choose two pieces of work that you are most proud of that show your learning and how you achieved the learning.

Reflect

■ What have you learned about reading and writing opinion pieces?

■ What new ideas about games do you have after reading this unit?

Tell about your choices

■ Tell why you chose each piece and how it shows your learning.

My choices	I want this in my portfolio because...

61

It's a Mystery

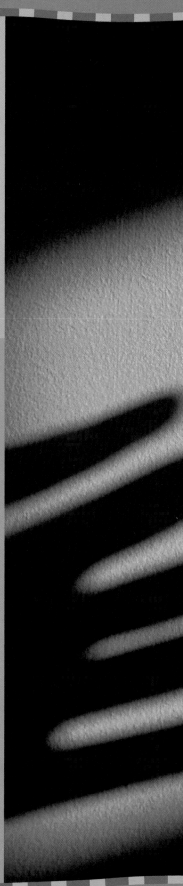

LEARNING GOALS

In this unit you will

- Solve mysteries you read and listen to by making inferences (thinking "between the lines").

- Learn techniques that mystery writers use to keep their readers interested.

- Create and share your own mysteries.

- Ask questions and discuss ideas about mysteries you and other people enjoy.

suspense
detective
puzzles
clues
evidence
eyewitness

by Aaron Rudolph

THE MYSTERY OF THE BERMUDA TRIANGLE

What Is the Bermuda Triangle?

The Bermuda Triangle lies in the Atlantic Ocean between the southeastern coast of Florida and the islands of Puerto Rico and Bermuda. An imaginary line connecting these three locations forms a triangle that covers an area a little larger than the province of Ontario.

The Bermuda Triangle is one of the most mysterious places in the world. Hundreds of planes, ships, and boats have disappeared in the Triangle. Many ship crews and pilots have reported strange happenings in the area.

> **What is mysterious about the Bermuda Triangle?**

The imaginary outline of the Bermuda Triangle is drawn over a map of the western Atlantic Ocean.

The Bermuda Triangle has inspired many stories in science fiction magazines.

The Start of a Legend

One of the first reports of odd happenings in the Bermuda Triangle occurred in 1492. Christopher Columbus and his crew sailed in the Bermuda Triangle on their way to North America. Columbus reported that his compass showed unusual readings in the area, and his crew also noticed a light in the sky.

After Columbus's journey, other sailors told stories about the Bermuda Triangle. Such stories are still told today.

Lost and Abandoned Ships

Disappearances of large ships in the Bermuda Triangle were common in the 1800s and early 1900s. Some ship crews also disappeared.

Atalanta

In 1880, the British ship *Atalanta* began a journey from Bermuda to England with about 300 people aboard. The ship failed to reach England. Rescue crews searched for it, but no trace of the ship or its crew was ever found.

Several people suggested reasons why the ship was not found. One theory was that a storm or a collision with an iceberg caused the *Atalanta* to sink.

Cyclops

In March 1918, the *Cyclops* disappeared in the Bermuda Triangle. The 165-metre-long navy ship was travelling from Barbados to the United States and carried more than 300 people. Many reasons for the disappearance were offered. Since this was the time of World War I, some stories said a weapon from a German submarine hit the *Cyclops*. Another story said the ship's captain sailed to Germany and gave up the crew to the Germans. The navy proved that this story was not true. The story of the *Cyclops* remains a mystery.

The *Spray*, shown above, was sailed by a Nova Scotian named Joshua Slocum. Both Slocum and the *Spray* disappeared in the Bermuda Triangle in 1909.

Lost and Unusual Flights

Ship stories are not the only Bermuda Triangle legends. Planes also vanish in the area, and pilots often report equipment problems.

Flight 19

One of the most famous aircraft disappearances in the Bermuda Triangle happened in 1945. On December 5th, five pilots in Avenger torpedo bombers left their air base in Florida on a training mission called Flight 19. After about two hours, the group's leader called the air base to say he was lost and that his compass had failed. Air traffic controllers tried to guide the pilots back on course, but the pilots' radio messages could not be heard clearly.

About three hours later, the base lost contact with the pilots. Rescue planes were sent after the group. One of these rescue planes also disappeared. No wreckage from the five Avengers or the rescue plane was ever found.

Avenger torpedo bombers, similar to those that disappeared

The Disappearing DC-3s

In December 1948, pilot Bob Linquist was flying a DC-3 airplane with 31 passengers over the Bermuda Triangle. He planned to land at the Miami airport, and told the air traffic controllers that he was approaching the runway. He was never heard from again. No one claimed to see or hear an explosion, and no wreckage was ever found.

In 1978, another DC-3 airplane disappeared in the Bermuda Triangle. It was flying from Florida to Cuba. The plane had gone about half the distance to Cuba when air traffic controllers noticed the plane had suddenly disappeared from their screens. Search crews never found the DC-3.

Looking for Answers

Researchers try to explain the events in the Bermuda Triangle. They study each case to find a cause. They also try to find a common cause for the events.

Weather

Many people think that weather causes some odd events in the Triangle. Weather in the area can change quickly. Clouds can make it hard for pilots and ship crews to see. Rain and thick clouds can affect instruments on ships and planes. High winds blowing from opposite directions can destroy small planes.

Ocean Features

Natural ocean occurrences can cause some ships to sink. Areas of swirling water called whirlpools can sink small ships. Underwater earthquakes may create large waves that can cause ships to fill with water and sink.

Other Theories

Some people believe human error causes most Bermuda Triangle disappearances. Other researchers say mines left behind from times of war sank some ships. One scientist believes magnetic forces may exist in the Triangle. He believes these forces can cause equipment failures, lights, or fog.

An Ongoing Legend

Many well-known disappearances in the Triangle happened more than 30 years ago. Today, better equipment helps captains and pilots stay on course and communicate, but planes and ships continue to disappear.

The Bermuda Triangle has puzzled people for hundreds of years. People will continue to wonder what causes the disappearances and strange events there until the mystery is solved.

Waterspouts can destroy any small craft in their way. They occur quite often in the Bermuda Triangle.

LET'S TALK ABOUT IT...

- Could there be other solutions to this mystery? Brainstorm some other possible explanations.

- The Bermuda Triangle is a real-life mystery. What other real-life mysteries do you know about?

Read Mystery Stories

Readers who enjoy mystery stories like to discover clues and piece together the evidence. They try to solve the mystery before the writer gives the solution.

TALK ABOUT IT!

Think about a favourite mystery story.

Tell a partner about the story.

- What was the mystery?
- What clues did the writer give?
- How well did the writer keep you guessing?
- What kind of mystery story was it?

What other kinds of mystery stories do you know about? What examples can you give? Here are some clues.

Make a chart together.

Reading Mysteries

Kinds of mysteries	Examples
– real-life	– Bermuda Triangle

Think Like a Reader

My hair stood on end as I watched the mysterious figure creep through the curtain of fog.

Read with a purpose

- Why do you read mystery stories?

Crack the code

Writers often use unusual expressions to catch their readers' interest. Sometimes the words don't mean exactly what they say. What "word picture" does this sentence paint? How would you explain, in everyday language, what the writer meant?

Make meaning

Three strategies you can use when reading mysteries are:

PREDICT Look at the title and pictures. Think about what you know about mystery stories.

INFER Read between the lines to figure out the clues. What's really happening?

CONNECT Think about how the story connects to other stories you have read or seen.

Analyze what you read

- How realistic are most of the characters in a mystery?
- What characteristics do mystery writers usually give to the "bad guys"?

THE STRANGEST FRIEND

Lina loved to relax on the deck of her house in Curve Lake. Everyone knew this was her favourite spot, but they didn't know why. Sure, she liked to look at the beautiful flowers in her mother's garden. She also liked to watch the many birds that came to the birdbath in the backyard. She liked them all except the big crow that showed up almost every day. He always made such a racket and chased the other birds away!

But the main reason Lina liked sitting on the deck was that somebody had started leaving presents for her there. The gifts were nothing fancy, but each one was something bright and shiny. The gift was always sitting on the railing right beside her chair. The first was a piece of aluminum foil. Lina picked it up and turned it over. The foil was warm from the sun, and Lina got the feeling that someone had left it there just for her.

PREDICT

Who do you think the "strangest friend" might be?

70

Two days later, she found a silver hairclip in the same spot. The next week, she found a quarter, and a couple of days later, a rhinestone ring.

Wow, she thought. *Somebody really likes me.*

When she questioned her mom about it, her mom seemed truly surprised.

"No, it isn't me," she said, "although I do love you very much."

Next, Lina asked her best friend, Tasha.

"Are you kidding?" said Tasha. "Why would I do something like that?"

Then Lina got a great idea. Taking a bag of flour from the kitchen, she spread some flour on the ground around the deck.

This way, I'll see the person's tracks, she thought, *and I can follow them.*

The next day, Lina found another present. This time it was a silver key for a bicycle lock. But looking at the flour around the deck, Lina couldn't see a single footprint! How could that be? Then she heard a sharp cry—Caw! Caw! Caw! That big crow was perched on the clothesline and was looking right at her. Its feathers were gleaming in the sunlight, and it seemed to be trying to tell her something.

"I wonder…," said Lina. "No, it couldn't be."

The crow gave one more cry before flying off to the south. Lina never saw it again. The strange thing, too, is that she never found another present on the railing.

INFER

Who do you think is leaving Lina the presents?

CONNECT

How does this story remind you of other stories you know?

71

THE ABANDONED HOUSE

My grandfather Sean likes to tell scary stories to see if he can frighten me. He says all of his stories are true, but sometimes I wonder. Here is one of his favourites.

When my grandfather was young, he and his closest friend, Dominic, lived down the street from an abandoned house. The house was situated on an overgrown lot and had been empty for years. All the windows were broken and the front door hung open, so anybody could go in and walk around. People in the neighbourhood said they could sometimes see lights in the house at night and shadows on the walls, as if someone was moving around inside. Sean and Dominic occasionally walked through the old house during the day, but they never saw anything suspicious. Finally, Dominic suggested coming back at night, but Sean thought that would be too frightening.

"All right," said Dominic. "Let's try at twilight, when it's not completely dark out yet."

"Okay," said Sean, "but bring a powerful flashlight. It might be dark by the time we leave."

They reached the house just as it was getting dark. In the first room they entered, they found someone had written a strange word on the wall with chalk: " ."

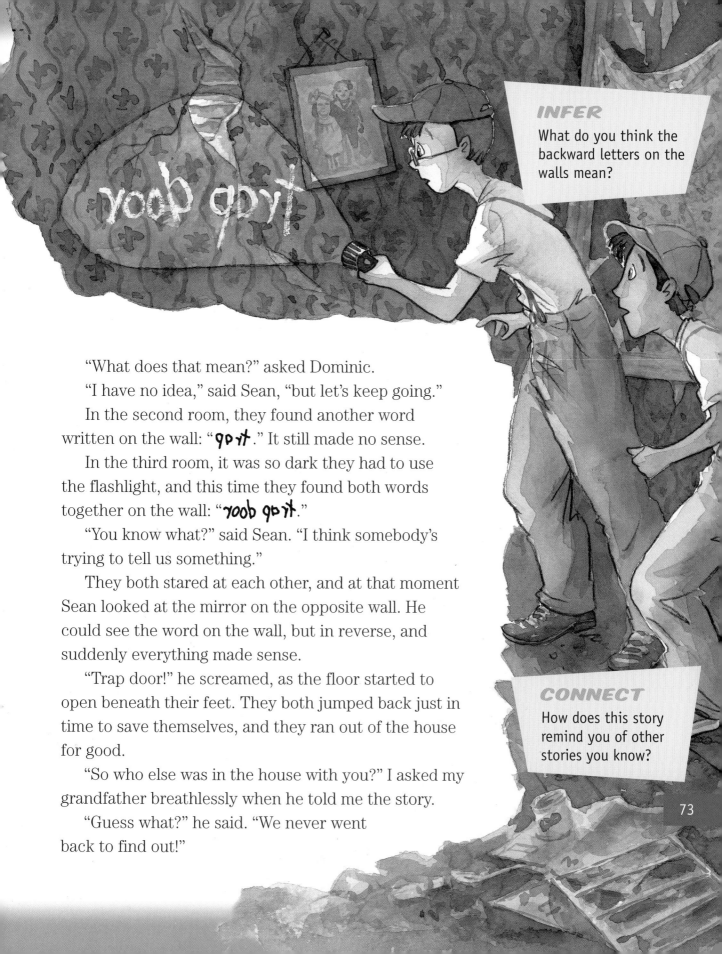

INFER

What do you think the backward letters on the walls mean?

"What does that mean?" asked Dominic.

"I have no idea," said Sean, "but let's keep going."

In the second room, they found another word written on the wall: "ꟼ૦ɤ." It still made no sense.

In the third room, it was so dark they had to use the flashlight, and this time they found both words together on the wall: "ɤ૦૦b ꟼ૦ɤ."

"You know what?" said Sean. "I think somebody's trying to tell us something."

They both stared at each other, and at that moment Sean looked at the mirror on the opposite wall. He could see the word on the wall, but in reverse, and suddenly everything made sense.

"Trap door!" he screamed, as the floor started to open beneath their feet. They both jumped back just in time to save themselves, and they ran out of the house for good.

"So who else was in the house with you?" I asked my grandfather breathlessly when he told me the story.

"Guess what?" he said. "We never went back to find out!"

CONNECT

How does this story remind you of other stories you know?

73

THE **CASE** OF THE
RUBY EARRINGS

The town of Harper's Landing was in an uproar. Somebody had broken into the house of Dr. Bannerfield, the richest man in town. Somehow, the thief had gotten away with the ruby earrings Dr. Bannerfield meant to give his wife, Susannah, for her birthday. The earrings were so valuable that Dr. Bannerfield had insured them for half a million dollars.

Police Detective Talia Hitchcock arrived at the Bannerfield home to find the doctor and his wife in the library, giving statements to Officer Dirk Magee. Ian Woodhouse, the family butler, was also present.

"Fill me in, Dirk," said Detective Hitchcock.

"This is a tough one, Boss," said Officer Magee. "The burglary took place in the middle of the night. Everyone had gone to bed, and nobody heard a thing. Looks like the burglar jimmied the lock on that window to get inside."

Detective Hitchcock turned to Dr. Bannerfield. "With such valuables in the house," she said, "I assume you have a good alarm system. Why didn't the alarm go off?"

PREDICT

What mystery might involve a pair of ruby earrings?

"Actually, Detective, we have no alarm," said the doctor. "I always thought our Rottweiler, Fang, would be enough to discourage any burglar. Not only does Fang have a vicious bite, but his bark is loud enough to wake anyone. We kept him locked in this room with the earrings all night."

When Detective Hitchcock asked what went wrong, the butler spoke up.

"We're not sure, Detective," he said. "I was awake for most of the night with a bout of insomnia. I never heard the dog bark once."

"Must have been a very skilled burglar," said Detective Hitchcock. "But I'm still surprised that you never invested in an alarm system."

"Oh, don't mention investments," said Susannah. "With the stock market collapsing, our investments are doing so poorly we have to pinch pennies wherever we can."

"I see," said Detective Hitchcock. "Pinching pennies but buying ruby earrings in the meantime. Officer Magee, arrest Dr. Bannerfield for pinching his wife's earrings to get the insurance money."

"How could you think I did it?" exclaimed Dr. Bannerfield.

"Because if it had been a stranger, your dog would have barked. But he knew you, so he never barked once!"

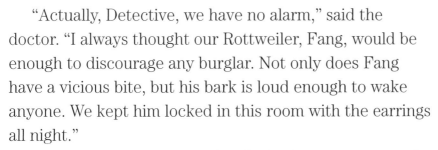

INFER

What do you think happened to the earrings?

CONNECT

How does this story remind you of other stories you know?

75

Reflect on Your Reading

I like to read mystery stories because I like finding clues to solve the mysteries. What about you?

You have . . .

- read "What's the Mystery?" mystery stories.
- talked about finding clues and gathering evidence.
- explored words and phrases that are related to mystery stories.

suspense   eyewitness   puzzles

detective   clues   evidence

You have also . . .

- explored three reading strategies.

PREDICT
INFER
CONNECT

Write About Learning

To solve a mystery, readers have to make inferences. They read between the lines to try to figure out what is really going on.

What strategies did you use to try to solve the mysteries? Write about how you used the writer's clues to solve one of the mysteries. Tell how finding clues helps you to read other stories.

Read Like a Writer

In a mystery, the words used to describe the mood, setting, characters, and events are very carefully chosen. These words help the reader feel, hear, and see the action as it unfolds. Sometimes the mood is suspenseful, and other times it is serious or humorous.

TALK ABOUT IT!

Look at the mysteries you have read. Include mysteries from your classroom library.

- Find words and phrases the writer uses to create pictures in your mind.
- Record other words the writer could have used.

HINT!

Look at how writers choose **words** and **phrases** to create pictures and feelings for their readers.

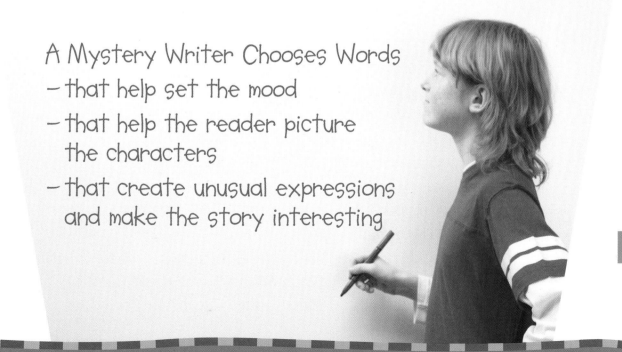

A Mystery Writer Chooses Words
- that help set the mood
- that help the reader picture the characters
- that create unusual expressions and make the story interesting

The Case of the Sneak

by Hy Conrad

Illustrated by Tina Holdcroft

How can you catch a sneak thief in sneakers?

It was Saturday afternoon and Tim and Lucy were playing space aliens in the woods. "Something's different," Tim said as they took a break between battles. "I know. Mr. Reed's not practising."

Mr. Reed was the school's music teacher. The woods lay right by his property and every Saturday, as Tim and Lucy played, the young cousins were always serenaded by solo clarinet music coming from the shack behind Mr. Reed's house.

Lucy climbed down from the tree house they were using as their star cruiser. "You're right. I hope nothing's wrong." The words were barely out of her mouth when they heard a distant shout. "That's him!"

Tim and Lucy ran to the edge of the woods. In front of them was Mr. Reed's field. In the middle of the field was the shack. Mr. Reed was there, peering through the shack's open door.

Thief's Sneakers

"I've been robbed!" he shouted for the fourth time. "Tim. Lucy. Hello." He was trying to control his anger. "I'd just unlocked the door when I noticed a split reed on my clarinet. I went back to my house to get a new one. I left the shack unlocked, just for a few minutes. And now look."

Tim and Lucy had never seen the inside before, but they'd heard about it. Mr. Reed's music shack had been burgled last year, and everything was stolen. When the music teacher brought in new furniture, he bolted it all to the floor—the table in the centre, the single chair by the table, even the filing cabinets.

At first glance, nothing seemed out of place. But then Lucy saw the pieces of broken pink pottery on the table. "Someone broke open your piggy bank?"

Mr. Reed looked embarrassed. "It held my rare silver dollar collection." He crossed the room and stretched his tall frame up to the blank space on his only shelf. "I kept it right here."

"A crime of opportunity," Tim said, as if he dealt with this every day. "The thief saw the unlocked door and was looking for something to steal. He or she grabbed the piggy bank, broke it open on the table—"

"Look," Lucy interrupted. "Footprints. Those aren't yours, are they?"

"No," Mr. Reed replied, examining the path of prints on the dusty floor. "I haven't been in here since last Saturday. Being in the middle of a field, this place gets dusty pretty fast."

READ LIKE A WRITER
Find different words and expressions the writer used instead of repeating "robbed."

79

Very carefully, Tim followed the prints, from the door over to the shelf, then back to the table. After that, a jumble of prints led all around the room. "I wonder what the thief was doing?"

Lucy was on the other side of the shack by a pair of nailed-down filing cabinets. "These look like knee prints," she said, pointing to a pair of round impressions between the cabinets. "Why would the thief kneel down?" She knelt down in the two knee prints. Right away, a glint of metal between the two cabinets caught her eye. Lucy reached her arm through the narrow gap and pulled out a silver dollar. "The thief was trying to reach this," she said proudly and handed the rescued coin to Mr. Reed. "He or she was wearing SkyMaster sneakers."

Tim stood up and wiped a little floor dust from his nose. "It's printed on the tread. Don't worry, Mr. Reed. We'll find your thief."

Tim and Lucy got on the case immediately. This was a lot more fun than fighting space aliens.

Their first stop was Garvey's, the only shoe store in town. Mr. Garvey informed them that SkyMaster was a new brand of sneakers.

"Since getting them in last week, I've made three sales," he said, checking his computer. "The first pair went to Todd Jones. Do you know him?"

"Sure," Lucy said. Everybody knew Todd "Beanpole" Jones. He resembled a two-metre-tall skeleton and was the centre of the high school basketball team.

"I sold the second pair to Ollie Infree. You kids probably don't know Ollie."

But they did. Ollie Infree was a petty criminal whose short height and taste for red suits made him look like a fire hydrant. He'd been arrested several times, once on Tim's and Lucy's suggestion. But he always managed to avoid conviction.

The third pair had been bought by Mona Everest, a human mountain, as tall as Beanpole and as stocky as Ollie. Mona had made a career for herself as a professional wrestler. Two years ago, she retired from the ring and moved to Harbourville in order to breed toy poodles.

"We'll have to spy on them all," Lucy whispered as they left the store.

"We're not spying on anyone," Tim insisted. "I think I already know who the culprit is."

Can you solve the case? Whom does Tim suspect? Todd, Ollie, or Mona?

DIG DEEPER

1. Make a story map. List the setting (when and where it happened), characters, and events of the story.
2. Choose part of the mystery to role-play with a group. Consider having one or more narrators read the words while others act out what is happening.

Characters	Setting
Problem	
Events	
Solution	

81

For the solution to this mystery, please turn to page 187.

The Game Master's Challenge:

What could be mysterious about a video game?

Cast

Narrator	storyteller
Dennis	10-year-old boy; rather cautious personality
Randy	friend of Dennis; somewhat daring personality
The Game Master	mysterious video game host

READ LIKE A WRITER

What words and phrases does the scriptwriter use to create suspense?

ACT 1: A COOL GAME

Narrator: It's one of those regular Saturday afternoons—at least, it started out that way. Dennis is at his computer playing his Mazecrawler game and keeps glancing anxiously at the clock.

Dennis: *(disappointed)* Maybe Randy forgot he was supposed to come over with a new game *(sigh)*—or maybe he's just late.

Narrator: Just then, a banging screen door and footsteps thundering up the stairs announce Randy's arrival. *(screen door bangs; thundering footsteps up the stairs)* Randy blazes into Dennis's bedroom, whipping off his backpack. He takes out a CD and triumphantly holds it up for Dennis's inspection.

Randy: *(excitedly)* Check this out!

Narrator: Dennis peers quizzically at the CD cover and notices it's black with a lightning bolt across it. He reads the name.

Dennis: "Realm of the Game Master." I've never heard of that game.

Randy: Me neither, but I found it at a neat little store on Sixth Street. The guy said this is the coolest game ever made! Since it's the test version, he gave it to me for free! C'mon, let's play!

A Radio Play
Adapted by Lynn Bryan
Illustrated by Peter Lacalamita

ACT 2: THE CHALLENGE

Narrator: Dennis pops the disk into his CD drive and waits patiently for the game to install. *(pause)* Instead, the screen goes completely black and then a thin, pale face, with no hair, not even eyebrows, gradually appears.

Dennis: *(uneasily)* I don't like the way that ugly face keeps looking right at me—it gives me the willies!

The Game Master: *(spooky background music) (eerie voice)* I am the Game Master. I challenge you to enter my mysterious realm. *(pause)* If you dare, click on the green shield and be taken on an amazing adventure. But beware: There is only one way out! Are you clever enough and brave enough to discover the secret? *(eerie laugh)*

Dennis: *(frightened)* This is too weird. Let's…

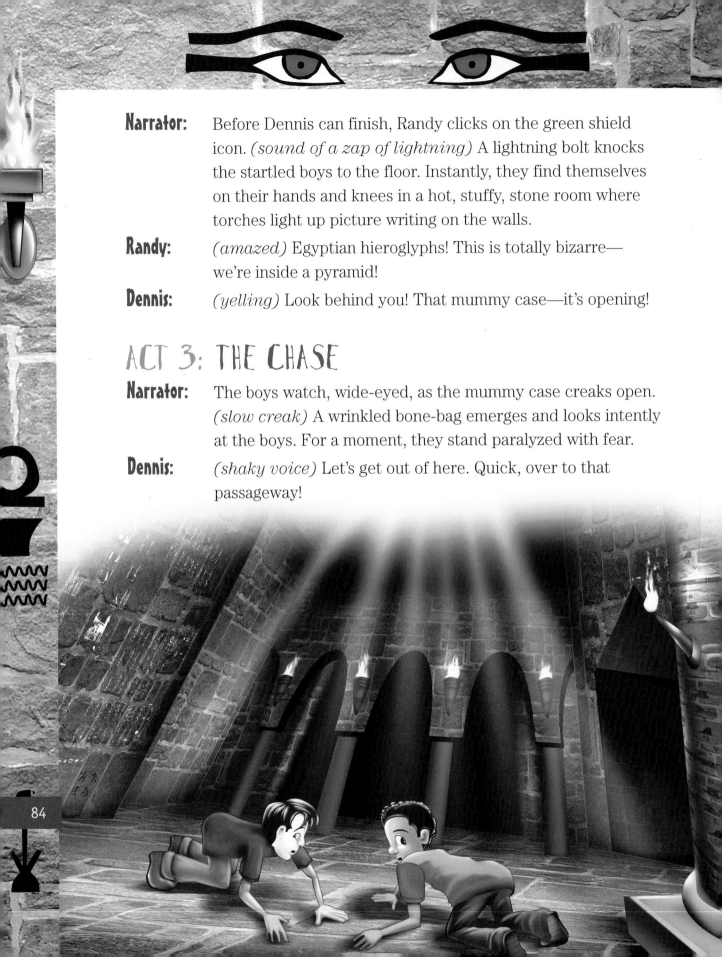

Narrator: Before Dennis can finish, Randy clicks on the green shield icon. *(sound of a zap of lightning)* A lightning bolt knocks the startled boys to the floor. Instantly, they find themselves on their hands and knees in a hot, stuffy, stone room where torches light up picture writing on the walls.

Randy: *(amazed)* Egyptian hieroglyphs! This is totally bizarre— we're inside a pyramid!

Dennis: *(yelling)* Look behind you! That mummy case—it's opening!

ACT 3: THE CHASE

Narrator: The boys watch, wide-eyed, as the mummy case creaks open. *(slow creak)* A wrinkled bone-bag emerges and looks intently at the boys. For a moment, they stand paralyzed with fear.

Dennis: *(shaky voice)* Let's get out of here. Quick, over to that passageway!

Narrator: Dennis and Randy turn and run—right into one another. Stumbling, they enter the dimly lit passageway and head down it. *(quick breathing as they run; padded footsteps in the distance, and getting closer)*

Randy: *(panting)* I hear footsteps behind us—the mummy is chasing us! Run faster!

Narrator: The boys continue running until the passageway suddenly divides and goes in two directions. At that moment, a furry grey creature scurries across one of the paths.

Randy: *(with a scream)* Eeeew, a rat!

Dennis: It's probably only a mouse… but I still don't like it. Let's head in the other direction!

Narrator: In a wild panic, the boys dash down the passageway, only to be met by an unexpected dead end in front of two huge wooden doors. The boys look frantically at one another.

Randy: *(desperately)* Let's try this one!

ACT 4: ANOTHER ADVENTURE

Narrator: The boys struggle against the heavy door. *(grunting sound)* Behind it, they discover what looks like a room in a medieval castle. Leaning against each wall is a huge suit of armour, complete with a battle sword and shield.

Randy: You know what's happened, don't you?

Dennis: Yeah. Somehow we've been transported into the game, but there's *got* to be a way out! Let's try the other door.

Narrator: *(clanging)* The sound of clanging metal stops them abruptly.

Dennis: Look! The red suit of armour is walking toward us!

Randy: *(frantically)* The others are coming, too. *(more clanging)* They're going to surround us! *(louder)* And look, there's a mouse crawling on your shoe! That Game Master creep said there was only one way out. We *have* to find it!

Narrator: *(suspenseful)* The knights are definitely closing in. *(pause)* To add to the tension, the mouse is now starting to crawl up Dennis's pant leg!

Dennis: *(hollering)* Aw, man! Get this mouse off me! *(pause)* Hey! *(pause)* That gives me an idea… *(hesitantly)* No, that can't really be the way out; it's too corny!

Randy: *(quickly)* Who cares? If you have an idea, go for it!

ACT 5: THE NOTE

Narrator: Dennis reaches down and picks up the squirming mouse.

Dennis: *(quietly)* Green means go, so… red must mean stop.

Narrator: Dennis turns to the red knight, holds the mouse up to its shield, and makes a clicking sound with his tongue. *(clicking)* Instantly, a flash of lightning fills the room. *(zapping sound)*

Randy: Hey, we're back in your room!

Dennis: *(disgusted)* The secret was a *really sick joke*. To start the game, we mouse-clicked on a green shield, right? So to get out…

Randy: You clicked a mouse on a red shield! *(groans)*

Dennis: Aw, man! Let's toss this disk!

Narrator: Dennis opens his CD drive but, to his amazement, the disk has disappeared.

Dennis: How can that be? Let's beetle over to the store where you got this game.

Narrator: All the boys see when they get there is a vacant lot.

Randy: *(confused)* I don't get it. That store *really was* here!

Dennis: Hey, here's a note on the ground. *(pause)* It says: "You won. Therefore, I must make my game more challenging. Perhaps we shall meet again. Signed: The Game Master."

DIG DEEPER ·····························

1. List the clues in the story that hint at the mouse being the solution.
2. Work in groups to present the radio play. Remember to use sound effects.

The Clue Catchers

The Clue Catchers: Maria, Panna, Julian, and Dexter

by Liam O'Donnell
Illustrated by
Dave Whamond

How do detectives know where to look for clues?

Mysteries are all around us. Hidden clues are everywhere, just waiting to be discovered. My name is Julian. My friends and I love solving mysteries so much that they call us the Clue Catchers. The guy at the front of our class is Dennis Rose, the famous mystery author and our latest case.

> This is a very rare copy of the first book featuring the world's most famous fictional detective, Sherlock Holmes.

> If he's so famous, why haven't I heard of him?

> Because you never leave your computer long enough to read a book, Maria!

> We can always count on Julian's logical brain to give us the facts, right, Dexter?

> That's right, Panna. But even I've heard of Sherlock Holmes. He's a totally famous character. His books have been around since the 1800s.

Panna is a forensics expert and she has great science marks to prove it.

Looks like string or maybe wool from a sweater. Think it came from our thief?

I can't be sure until I look at it under the microscope in the science room.

This door was locked during recess, so the thief must have had keys to the classroom.

Only the teachers have keys.

Hanna, the caretaker, has keys too. I saw her standing near Mrs. Tanaka's desk during recess.

When we tracked down Hanna, she was having a stormy reunion with Mr. Rose.

Upset over your lost book, Dennis? You deserved it. Now you know how it feels to be robbed!

Are you still angry with me, Hanna? If you've taken my Sherlock Holmes book, you will pay!

How do they know each other?

I doubt they'd tell us. I'm going to check online to learn a little more about our mystery writer and our mysterious caretaker.

Good idea. Dexter, follow Mr. Rose when he leaves. I'm going to try to get some answers from Hanna.

Hanna admitted to being in the classroom during recess. She was emptying the garbage at the front of the class, but didn't notice the Sherlock Holmes book.

I did hear a thudding noise near the desk. When I turned around there was no one there. I finished cleaning and locked the door when I left the room.

If the thief was small, he or she could have hidden under the desk.

Outside, Dexter overheard Mr. Rose on the phone to his publisher. If he was upset about losing his Sherlock Holmes book, he wasn't showing it.

Call the newspapers, Trish! This theft will be great publicity for my new mystery novel.

In the science room, Panna was getting closer to identifying the yellow fibres.

Check this out, Maria. These fibres are too smooth to be string or to come from a wool sweater. My guess is that they're some type of ribbon.

Do you know what happened to the book? Watch out for false clues!

SOLUTION

Clues

- Theresa stayed behind in the classroom to look at the book. Later, she was supposed to be helping in the library, but Mrs. Tanaka couldn't find her.
- After the theft, the ribbon on Theresa's badge was ripped. The yellow fibres found on the desk matched the ribbon on the badge. Only Theresa was small enough to fit under the desk.
- Hanna heard a thudding noise near the desk while she was tidying the room.

Conclusion

While looking at the book, Theresa heard someone coming into the room and hid under the desk. Theresa then tried to slip the book back up onto the desk. However, she couldn't see very well, and didn't reach up far enough to put the book fully on the desk. The book fell into the garbage can, which Hanna then emptied without noticing the book. The Clue Catchers put the clues together and recovered the book. Dennis Rose was so impressed with the Clue Catchers' detective work that he promised to dedicate his next mystery novel to them.

DIG DEEPER

1. Pretend you are one of the characters in the story. What did your character think happened to the book? Why did he or she think that?

2. Imagine that you are a newspaper or TV reporter. Work with a partner to write a report on the crime.

Graphic Writers at Work!

Graphic writers create their work in a comic strip format. The story is written in sequence with each panel representing a part of the story. Speech bubbles hold the dialogue.

It's your turn to write a graphic story!

Brainstorm

- Brainstorm mystery stories that you might like to create as a graphic story. Or choose your own topic and imagine it as a story with pictures and dialogue.
- Share your topic with a classmate.

Organize Your Ideas

- Think about the characters. How will they look and act?
- Decide if you need a narrator or a text box in the corner to help explain the story.
- Visualize the story sequence before you start. Which scenes will have the most action? How will you illustrate movement?

94

Create Your Story

- Fold your paper into panels and sketch your thoughts and ideas.

Make It Better

- Read over your work. Think about it. Does your mystery make sense?
- Is there a beginning, middle, and end to your story?
- Are there visual clues for the reader to find?
- Do the illustrations and text work together?
- Share your draft with a classmate. Discuss possible changes.

Share Your Graphic Story

- Think of how to present your finished graphic story.

WAYS TO SHARE

- Create a class book of your stories.
- Post them in the school hallway for other classes to read.
- Make an e-book for the school library.

Imagine

What kind of night can you imagine?

a Night

by SARAH L. THOMSON

Illustrated by ROB GONSALVES

imagine a night . . .

. . . when the darkness

of meadow and lake

feels too quiet and deep,

and so you cut and stitch a city

from the starry sky.

DIG DEEPER

1. How does the artist create a mysterious mood?
2. Revisit one of the mystery stories or poems that you have read.
   Create an illustration for the story or poem to make it look and
   feel mysterious or suspenseful.

A Mysteriously Good Writer

by Allison Gertridge

How do writers create realistic stories?

Eric Wilson began his writing career when he was a teacher. "I was working with Grade 8 students in BC—kids who didn't like to read at all and didn't seem to know much about Canada. That's what gave me my two principal goals, which were to write about Canada and to write books that would get kids into reading."

Over the years, Eric has discovered the best way to reach those goals. "I select a location and go and live there, then try and work into my stories as many of my own personal experiences as possible."

Take for example his book *The Inuk Mountie Adventure*. In it, the character Tom Austen is on an exchange trip from Winnipeg, Manitoba, to Gjoa Haven, Nunavut. Eric joined a group of students on a winter exchange in that very same town. Eric made a special effort to get to know the people and their community. "Like the students, I stayed with a local family and so we got to eat caribou and that sort of thing. All those experiences [went] into my story."

Eric also carries a tape recorder on these excursions. That way, he dictates notes and records as much of the moment as he can.

"That, essentially, is what the research is; it's going to a real place and writing about it. That's why when I talk to kids in schools, I always say, if you're going to do a story, begin by writing about some place that you know, namely your own neighbourhood or your own town."

When the field work is complete, Eric takes all that raw data home. There he spends between two and four months assembling it, thinking about his characters, and sorting related information.

"For example, I'll have a scene that takes place at the school in Gjoa Haven, and so all the research that I did at the school I'll assemble in one file in my computer. Then when I come to do the actual writing, I'll go through that material and pick out what I think is the most interesting and telling information."

When it finally comes time to write the first draft of his new story, Eric will do the same thing he always does when he's writing. He cuts himself off from every distraction. "When I'm going to be writing, I switch off the phone, hang a Do Not Disturb sign on the door of my apartment, and close all of the curtains so that I cut off my beautiful view of the Pacific Ocean and the mountains. The only light on in my apartment is a little tiny light glowing over my computer keyboard so it's like a dark little cave. I like to be in that cave, so that when I'm writing my story, I'm in Gjoa Haven rather than in Victoria."

It takes Eric about two months to complete his first draft, working closely with his wife, Flo. He then prints it out ten times for what he describes as ten really important editors—five girls and five boys in Grades 4 through 8.

READ LIKE A WRITER Eric Wilson is careful about the words he uses in his writing. How do you know that?

"They take the story home with them and they keep a diary. At the end of each chapter, they stop and write down the answers to several questions for me, including who they think the villain is and why, because this is a test-read for the clues." Eric also asks them to let him know where he's used dated language and where they think the story gets boring. "In other words, those ten kids read the story on behalf of all the kids who will read it as a book."

Then, of course, Eric works on rewrites with his editor. After another couple of months of work, his manuscript is finally ready for his publisher. Not a bad system, really, since Eric's books have been wildly popular with thousands of kids across Canada and as far away as Spain and Japan.

MEDIA WATCH

Watch in magazines and newspapers for other author profiles. Who do you think benefits from stories like these?

DIG DEEPER

1. What is the author's opinion of Eric Wilson and his books? Read between the lines to find out! List the evidence you find.

2. Choose one of your favourite mystery books. Write a review telling what it is about and why you like it. Be sure to tell how other students can find the book.

Title:	Author:
What is it about?	
Why I like it:	

POEMS OF MYSTERY

Midnight

by sean o huigin
Illustrated by
Luc Melanson

there's a scratching
on the front porch
there's a sniffing
'round the door
someone's whining
in the darkness
i can't stand it
anymore
i peek out through
the curtains
and in the night
i see
two shining evil
looking eyes
staring back at me

the scratching's
getting louder
i can hear the beast
begin
to pant and huff
and push and shove
OH NO
it's gotten in
WOOF WOOF WOOF
pant pant pant

READ LIKE A WRITER

How do these poets use
descriptive language to
create a picture for their
readers?

Snow Woman

by Elizabeth Holden (age 10)
Illustrated by Luc Melanson

A winter's night,
And in the snow outside,
A snow woman forms.

Her icy fingers touch,
Her split snake tongue flickers,
Her evil eyes stare.

Her nails strike down trees,
Her eyes still, and mad.
Night creatures flee.

She grins,
Her laughter echoing.

As a splinter of light
Snatches at her gown
Her feet vanish,
Her ankles, knees, and thighs,
Her cackles silenced.

She grabs the empty air,
Her head sliding.
Her hand reaches one last time,
But she is gone.

DIG DEEPER

1. Who or what do you think is creating the mystery in each of these poems?

2. With a small group, write a mysterious poem. Think about what sound effects would add a sense of mystery to your poem.

How can people today solve mysteries from long ago?

The Mary Celeste

An Unsolved Mystery from History

BY JANE YOLEN AND

HEIDI ELISABET YOLEN STEMPLE

ILLUSTRATED BY ROGER ROTH

When I grow up I want to be a detective, just like my dad. He says I was born curious, which is just what a detective needs to be.

What I'm most curious about now is my father's file of old mysteries that have never been solved. They have baffled people for years. Dad calls these cases "open" but I call them "history mysteries," and I am determined to figure them out.

For each mystery, I read as much as I can about it. I keep a notebook in which I highlight the most important clues. Sometimes I draw a map and a timeline. And I always keep a list of important words that are special to the case to help me understand what happened.

READ LIKE A WRITER
How do the writers make the setting believable?

The Mary Celeste is about a ship whose crew disappeared when it was on the high seas more than a hundred and twenty years ago. The crew was never found. Though lots of people have ideas—or theories—about what might have happened, no one is sure. But Dad says no mystery is impossible to solve as long as you have enough clues.

This is how the story goes:

A brisk December wind filled the great sails of the *Dei Gratia.* She had left New York on November 15, 1872, to cross the cold Atlantic with a cargo of petroleum. It was a long trip, many days on an empty ocean, and nothing to look at but the thin line between sea and sky. Early in the afternoon of December 4 (December 5 in sea time), seaman John Johnson, alert at the wheel, spotted a smudge on the horizon. He called out excitedly, "Captain Morehouse, sir, there is something coming toward us off the port bow!"

Captain Morehouse looked through his spyglass. Even though the smudge was kilometres away, he could tell it was a ship heading in their direction. But as she came closer, he saw that the ship moved slowly, oddly, running aimlessly before the wind. Only three sails were still set. Two had been blown away, and one was lying loose. The rest of the sails were furled. Several of the *Dei Gratia*'s crew gathered at the rail to watch the oncoming brig. They all knew something was wrong.

"Get me Mr. Deveau," ordered the captain.

A seaman went below deck to rouse the first mate from his berth. By the time Deveau joined the captain, the other ship was near.

"Look!" Morehouse said, handing the mate the spyglass.

Deveau looked and saw no one on deck. "But," he said, "they fly no flag of distress. Perhaps they lie drunken below.

sea time

sea time and shore time are measured twelve hours apart because sea time is counted from noon, when the sun stands directly overhead

106

At the wheel, Johnson laughed. "They wouldn't if they had a captain like ours!"

Captain Morehouse laughed, too, then said, "Let us hail them."

They ran up the flags that offered help. Minutes went by and they got no reply. When they sailed closer still, the captain called out through his speaking trumpet. He was greeted by a strange silence.

"Something is definitely amiss," the captain said. "Someone must go over and see."

So a small boat was lowered. Three of the sailors— Deveau, Johnson, and second mate John Wright—rowed across to the silent brig.

The ship was a bit over thirty metres in length with an ornamental scroll on her bow.

"What is she called?" asked Johnson. He was pulling on the oars and so could not see. "The *Mary Celeste* out of New York," said Deveau, reading the name on her stern.

The only sounds were their own voices and the *slip-slap* of the waves. From the *Mary Celeste* there was silence.

Deveau and Wright clambered on board, leaving seaman Johnson behind. Slowly they searched from bow to stern, but there was no one up on the deck, not even at the ship's wheel. The wheel was neither damaged nor lashed to a single course. The lifeboat that should have been lying across the main hatch was missing. Wright and Deveau checked the ship's pumps, which turned out to be in good working order, and besides there was little water in the hold.

"Mutiny?" whispered Wright, as if afraid to say the word aloud. "Or a fever ship?"

"Maybe pirates," Deveau whispered back. "Let's go on."

The captain's cabin sat neat and shipshape, except that the bed had not yet been made—the print of a small body was on the covers—and several toys lay scattered on the floor. An old dress hung near the bed, some India rubber overshoes standing under it. In the water closet sat a bag of dirty clothing. A rosewood harmonium stood silent against one wall, above it a shelf of music books. The captain of the *Mary Celeste* had brought his family with him and many of the comforts of home.

In the first mate's cabin the ship's log lay open, the last entry dated 8:00 a.m., November 25. No trouble had been noted up to that time.

But some important items were missing from the *Mary Celeste*.

"Where is the chronometer?" asked Wright.

Deveau added, "And where are the sextant, navigation book, and ship's register?"

They both knew a ship would never sail without these. Had the captain taken them with him when he left? Then why had the family not taken their clothes or the captain's wife her jewellery? The two men asked themselves these questions.

mutiny
when a ship's crew revolts against the captain, usually killing him and taking over the ship

fever ship
a ship on which the crew have all taken ill or died from a disease, perhaps yellow fever or cholera

water closet
the ship's toilet

harmonium
a kind of musical instrument—a reed organ

chronometer
a very accurate ship's clock, not affected by motion or weather

sextant
an instrument used by sailors to navigate by the stars

There was nothing to eat or drink in the captain's cabin, so the sailors checked in the ship's galley and pantry. There they found a six-month supply of uncooked food and fresh water.

They checked the crew's quarters, which were in good order, except that there was no crew anywhere to be found.

The last place the men looked was in the ship's hold where her cargo—1700 barrels of raw alcohol—was well stowed. Not a single barrel had been opened. All in all, Deveau and Wright looked around the *Mary Celeste* for over half an hour. They found no sign of anyone on board, no signs of struggle.

The men did not speak as they rowed back, but once on board the *Dei Gratia,* they had much to say. The captain listened sadly to their report, for he knew Captain Briggs and his wife, Sarah. He had even had dinner with them at the Astor House before they sailed. They had told him their two-year-old daughter, Sophia, was travelling with them, but their seven-year-old son, Arthur, had been left behind to go to school. Captain Morehouse knew that Captain Briggs was a good sailor, a smart master, and fair to his crew.

"The men's oilskins, boots, and pipes were all left behind. The lady left her gold lockets. They went quickly, sir," said Deveau. "I do not think they meant to be gone for good." Then he added: "I propose we bring the *Mary Celeste* in for salvage. Now, by the laws of the sea, she belongs to us."

Captain Morehouse thought about salvaging the boat. "It will be dangerous for both ships. Our crew is small. I cannot spare more than three men."

Deveau nodded. "I can manage, sir," he said.

Deveau took only two sailors, a small boat, a barometer, a compass, and a watch, and rowed back across to the silent ship.

It took them several days to make the *Mary Celeste* seaworthy again, pumping out the small amount of water and fixing the sails and masts.

Then they sailed her to Gibraltar where Captain Morehouse and his crew had to defend their rights to the ship at a long and difficult salvage trial.

penny papers
the old name for tabloid newspapers because long ago they sold for a penny

That trial was big news, reported in all the penny papers of the day. The newsboys on the streets called out the latest gossip.

"Bloody sword found on *Mary Celeste*!"

"Planks in splinters from a fight!"

"Half-eaten breakfast still on the table!"

"Thirteen missing from cursed ship!"

Readers thrilled to these stories, but some were half-truths and some were outright lies.

The only people who knew what really happened on the *Mary Celeste,* after the last log entry had been written, were the ten people on board. They could have told the real story if they had ever been found.

They never were.

So what DID happen? My dad says no one knows for sure. But now that you have read the story, maybe you can solve the mystery of the *Mary Celeste*. Perhaps you will think one of the old theories is how things really happened. Or maybe you'll come up with a theory of your own.

Only remember, as my dad always says, *Check Your Clues*.

DIG DEEPER

1. With a partner, come up with a theory that explains what happened to the *Mary Celeste*. Research in books and on the Internet, and list your evidence. Present your theory to the class. Be convincing!

2. How did the writers mix fact and fiction in their story?

The Night Walker

Who is the Night Walker?

BY RICHARD THOMPSON
ILLUSTRATED BY MARTIN SPRINGETT

The boy went exploring late one afternoon.

He waded across the stream.

He climbed the hill.

He wandered through the forest.

He crossed the field of stones.

He followed a winding path through the tall grass.

The boy went exploring late one afternoon—all the way to the watering hole.

The boy always carried a knobbly stick for poking into holes, and for helping him balance on steep places, and just in case. And he always carried, tied to his belt, a pouch that he could close by pulling on a string—to collect his treasures in.

On this late afternoon, the boy found a nail and three coins. He put those treasures in his pouch. In the forest he found a smooth, green rock and a small piece of wood that looked like a man running. Among the stones in the field of stones, he found a feather that might have been an eagle's feather. Near the watering hole, he found a few dried leaves from a sweet-breath bush. His mother would like those leaves.

The boy was so intent on looking for treasures to put in his pouch that he didn't notice the sun going down. And then it was dark, and the boy was a long way from home.

He started back through the tall grass. The night was full of sounds. He could hear an owl calling. He could hear insects churring and whirring. He could hear—and then not quite hear—the sighing song of the night breeze. And then, he realized he could hear something else…

READ LIKE A WRITER

How does the writer repeat words and phrases to build suspense?

…a clinking sound,
a clicking sound,
a rustling sound…
very close by.
He stopped. He couldn't hear the something else
now—just the owl, and the insects, and the breeze.
He started walking again.

And now he could hear it again…
a clinking sound,
a clicking sound,
a rustling sound.
He stopped. The sound stopped. He walked. He could hear
the sound again.
Something was following him!

The boy told himself that it was a rabbit moving in the grass. A rabbit was nothing to be afraid of. But maybe it was something bigger…

Maybe it was a wild dog or a fox. A wild dog or a fox was nothing to be afraid of. He had his knobbly stick, just in case, and he could chase away a wild dog or a fox.

But he walked faster. And whateveritwas walked faster.

It might be a panther. The boy walked faster again. And whateveritwas walked faster again.

Or it might be a bear.

Or it might be one of those creatures in the stories that told you to never-go-out-in-the-night-alone—a Night Walker!

A Night Walker had long, sharp claws. And the boy could hear them clicking against the stones on the path!

A Night Walker carried a sack. And the boy could hear the rustling sound of the boy-catching sack dragging along the ground!

A Night Walker had bits of chains around its ankles because it had been chained in a dark place, and it had broken loose to wander. The boy could hear the bits of chain clinking!

A knobbly stick would not scare a Night Walker.

The boy started to run. And he could hear the Night Walker running right behind him.

He ran faster. And he could hear the Night Walker clinking and clicking and rustling faster behind him.

He could hear the Night Walker's loud breathing! Any moment now, long, sharp claws would reach out of the dark and grab him.

All of a sudden, the boy was tumbling and tumbling. He had tripped on a stone or a root. His heart clenched as he waited for the Night Walker to pounce.

But when he stopped tumbling, all he could hear was the thunder of his blood and the tornado of his breathing.

And, as the storm of his fear blew away, the boy could hear no sound at all.

For a long time the boy listened.

He listened, and he heard no clinking sound.

He listened, and he heard no clicking sound.

He listened, and he heard no rustling sound.

But, eventually, he heard an owl call. He heard insects churring and whirring. And maybe the sound of the breeze.

Was the Night Walker gone, or was he standing and listening, too? The boy dared not move. He sat very still. And listened.

Eventually, though, the boy grew weary from the hard work of listening… and he fell asleep.

When the sun came up, the boy stood and looked around.

He was in the field of stones at the bottom of the short slope he had tumbled down in the dark. Nearby lay his knobbly stick. His pouch had come undone and was lying on the ground. The boy picked up the stick and the pouch, and started quickly for home.

Birds were singing, and the boy sang, too.

The boy sang as he hurried through the field of stones.

He sang as he hurried through the forest.

He sang as he hurried over the hill and across the stream.

He sang, but he hurried, because he knew that his mother would be very angry.

But the boy's mother was so happy to see him home and safe that she forgot about being angry.

The boy's mother hugged him and said, "Tell me your story."

The boy told his story. About how he had wandered too far, and how the sun had gone down, and how the whateveritwas had followed him and changed from a rabbit into a wild dog and from a wild dog into a panther, and how the boy had known that it was really a Night Walker.

He told about how the Night Walker had chased him, and how he had fallen.

When the story was finished, the boy showed his mother the treasures he had found.

"A nail and three coins…" They made a soft clinking sound as they tumbled from his hand.

"A smooth, green rock and a piece of wood that looks like a man running…" He laid them down. They made a very small clicking sound.

"And a feather and some dried leaves from a sweet-breath bush. The leaves are for you, Mother." The leaves rustled as he spread them out.

His mother smiled. "You know, my boy," she said, "sometimes the monster you hear behind you in the dark is only the clink and click and rustle of the things you have collected during the day."

"Or it might be the Night Walker," said the boy.

"True," said his mother. "It might be the Night Walker."

DIG DEEPER ••

1. Think of a song that would be good background music if this story was made into a movie. Share your ideas with the class.

2. Write a story similar to this one, but in a different setting.

Connect and Share

You've read and talked about mystery stories at school. Now it's time to find out about mystery stories your family and friends enjoy!

Ask questions at school and at home

- With a partner or in a group, brainstorm some questions you could ask your classmates about mystery stories they enjoy.
- Choose two questions to ask.
- Ask three people at school.
- Ask the same questions at home.
- Record the answers.

IDEAS FOR QUESTIONS

- Do you like mystery stories? Why?
- Would you rather read or watch a mystery?
- What are some of your favourite mysteries?
- What real-life mysteries do you know about?

Bring ideas back!

- Meet with a group.
- Make a list, chart, or graph to show what you found out.

Spotlight on Learning

Collect

- Gather your notebooks, your writing, and your projects from this unit.

Talk and reflect

Work with a partner.

- Together, read the Learning Goals on page 62.
- Talk about how well you met these goals.
- Look through your work for evidence.

Select

- Choose two pieces of work that show how you achieved the Learning Goals. (The same piece of work can show more than one goal.)

Tell about your choices

- Tell what each piece shows about your learning.

My choices	I want this in my portfolio because...

Reflect

- What have you learned during your study of mysteries?
- What have you discovered about the techniques that mystery writers use?

121

We Are Canadian!

LEARNING GOALS

In this unit you will

- Read and listen to stories, songs, poems, and information about Canada.

- Summarize information you read, view, and hear.

- Present ideas and information orally and through drama.

- Write, illustrate, and share information about Canada's peoples, celebrations, and symbols.

official symbols
coat of arms
contributions
celebrations
citizenship
diversity

Canada in

What symbols best represent Canada to you?

Maple leaves are famous Canadian symbols, like the ones stamped on the penny.

Chorus:

I've got Canada in my pocket, a little bit of history
A penny, and a nickel, and a quarter, and a dime
Mean a lot to you and me
It's more than pocket money
They're the symbols of our land
They're pictures of important things
For which this country stands

124

My Pocket

A song by Michael Mitchell

Since 1851, the beaver has been a Canadian symbol. It's on the nickel.

The maple leaf, the maple leaf is a beautiful sight to see
It waves "hello" to us below, from the branch of a maple tree
And with every year that passes, it grows like you and me
So should we all grow straight and tall
Like the lovely maple tree

Chorus

The beaver, oh the beaver, is a beautiful sight to see
He's a happy, furry animal, like a teddy bear with teeth
He's never, ever lazy, he works all night and day
Building houses for his family, he's got no time to play

Chorus

The schooner, oh the schooner, is a beautiful sight to see
It's a great big, wooden sailing ship
That can sail across the sea
It brings to other countries the things their people need
And brings back things like chocolate bars
And books for us to read

Chorus

The caribou, the caribou, is a beautiful sight to see
He's a really big, strong animal, I'm sure you'll all agree
He looks just like a reindeer
And he loves it when the wind blows cold
So he lives up north with the polar bears
'Cause he likes the ice and snow

Chorus

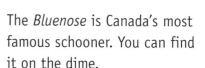

The *Bluenose* is Canada's most famous schooner. You can find it on the dime.

The caribou, an important animal for the Inuit and many First Nations peoples, is featured on the Canadian quarter.

Michael Mitchell is a popular singer, songwriter, and storyteller. He tours the country, visiting schools to perform his songs and tell his stories. It was through his visits to schools across the country that he got the idea to create a booklet and CD called *Canada Is For Kids*, which contains the song "Canada in My Pocket."

Here is what Michael had to say about why he made *Canada Is For Kids*:

Over my years of travelling and performing throughout Canada, I have come to realize that there is little opportunity for our younger citizens to share in the music of our land. In this booklet, I have put together a collection of Canadian songs to help our youth gain a glimpse of this country through musical windows into our heritage... I hope that this booklet, and my recordings, will encourage some kids (and maybe even some adults) to learn more about what this great country is all about.

LET'S TALK ABOUT IT...

- What other Canadian symbols can you think of? Why are they important to Canada?

- Sketch a symbol you would choose for a new Canadian coin or bill. Explain why you chose it.

127

Reading in Social Studies

Reading in Social Studies can help you learn about Canada and other countries. Think of a book or TV show about Canada that you've enjoyed.

TALK ABOUT IT!

- Tell a partner something important you learned about Canada from this book or TV show.

- Talk about the different places you can find information about Canada and other countries.

Here are some clues.

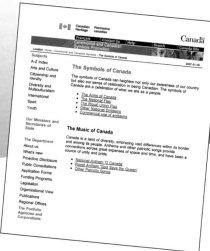

Make a chart together.

Learning About Canada and Other Countries

Where to find information	Examples

Light and Life

Inside the blue and gold circle are symbols that honour the traditional Inuit way of life. In the bottom left is a stone lamp, or *qulliq* (KUH-lik). This lamp provides light during the dark winter. It also represents the warmth of family and friends. Next to it is a stone marker called an *inuksuk* (ee-NOOK-sook). Inuit hunters built these markers as signposts to direct their way through the Arctic.

The North Star at the top of the circle has guided people in the Arctic for thousands of years. The star also represents the Elders, who lead and advise the people of Nunavut. The five gold circles around the star stand for the rising and setting of the sun.

The symbol above the circle is an iglu, a traditional shelter made of ice and snow. The crown on top of the iglu represents the Queen and shows that Nunavut is part of Canada. The Inuktitut words at the bottom, *Nunavut Sanginivut*, mean "Nunavut, our strength."

DECIDE WHAT'S IMPORTANT

What key points did you learn about Nunavut's coat of arms?

Elders are leaders and advisors in Nunavut.

SUMMARIZE

Organize the main ideas in a web.

Did You Know...?

The narwhal's long tusk is really a tooth that grows outward in a spiral. In the Middle Ages, explorers brought narwhal tusks to Europe and claimed they were horns from unicorns. Kings and queens would pay a lot for a horn. They believed it was magical.

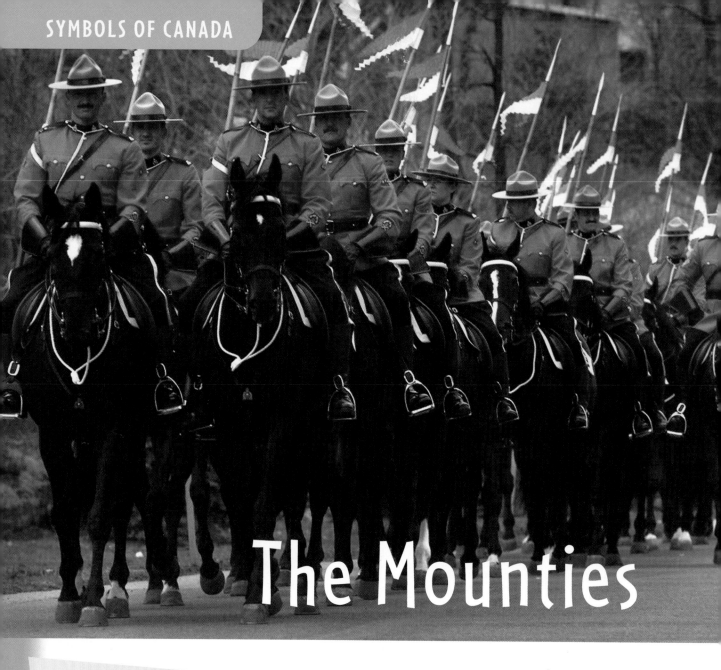

The Mounties

USE WHAT YOU KNOW

What do you know about the RCMP?

People around the world recognize the scarlet jacket, Stetson hat, and polished boots as symbols of Canada's national police force. Most people know these police officers as the Royal Canadian Mounted Police (RCMP). Canadians often refer to them as the Mounties. They represent Canada's idea of peace, justice, fairness, and order.

The Need for a Police Force

During the 1870s, the land that is now Alberta and Saskatchewan was part of a larger region called the North-West Territories. Changes were happening fast there. European settlers were claiming lands that were home to First Nations peoples. As more people came, crime increased. There were no police to enforce law and order.

The Canadian government took action. It called for men who were 18 to 40 years of age to join a new police force. The men had to be able to ride a horse, be of good character, and be strong and healthy. They also had to be able to read and write in French or English. In 1874, the North-West Mounted Police (NWMP) was formed.

Changes in the Police Force

Over the years, the NWMP expanded into other parts of Canada. In 1920, the force was renamed the Royal Canadian Mounted Police.

Today, this police force is as important as it was then. Both men and women from many cultures work as RCMP officers across Canada. Together, they work to keep law and order all over the country.

DECIDE WHAT'S IMPORTANT

What key points did you learn about the RCMP?

Today, men and women from many cultures work as RCMP officers.

SUMMARIZE

Organize the main ideas in a web.

Did You Know...?

The first recruits to the North-West Mounted Police were paid between $0.75 and $1.00 a day.

Reflect on Your Reading

You have . . .

- talked about some Canadian symbols.
- read and viewed information about Canada.
- explored words and phrases that tell about Canada.

government   traditional

territories   symbols

coat of arms   Parliament Hill

You have also . . .

- explored three reading strategies.

I like to learn about Canada's symbols because they have lots of history behind them. What about you?

USE WHAT YOU KNOW

DECIDE WHAT'S IMPORTANT

SUMMARIZE

Write About Learning

Which strategy did you find most helpful in reading one of the reports from the selection "Symbols of Canada"? Explain how you used it. How will this strategy help in reading other reports in Social Studies?

Read Like a Writer

The selections in "Symbols of Canada" are *reports*. Reports present information about specific topics, organized into paragraphs. Effective sentences are an important element of reports.

TALK ABOUT IT!

- What do you notice about the sentences in the reports?
- What conjunctions or linking words do you notice?
- Make a list of ways writers create effective sentences in reports.

HINT!

How does the writer vary the **sentences** to create interest?

Effective Sentences in a Report
- The sentences are different lengths.
- They start in different ways.
- Sentence parts are joined by linking words such as <u>but</u>, <u>who</u>, and <u>although</u>.

137

People Who Make a

by Brian Linden

How can people be symbols?

An Amazing Natural Athlete

There was a time when people thought it was not ladylike for women to take part in competitive sports. Some women, however, were willing to break this barrier.

Fanny "Bobbie" Rosenfeld was one of them. Bobbie is remembered as one of Canada's greatest all around athletes. She entered the competitive sports of track and field, tennis, basketball, softball, and hockey. Although she never had a coach, she was a champion in them all!

READ LIKE A WRITER
How does the writer use interesting ways to begin some sentences?

Bobbie won silver in the 100 m race at the 1928 Olympic Games.

138

Difference

Bobbie ran her first race as a child in Barrie, Ontario. At a town picnic, she and her sister lost their lunch money. Luckily, a race had been organized for children, with a box lunch as the prize. Bobbie entered and won!

Bobbie started competing in sports long before designers dreamed of creating sportswear for women. She recalled what she wore at the Canadian National Exhibition: "I finished the race wearing my brother's swimming trunks, dad's socks, and a gym jersey."

Bobbie reached her peak at the 1928 Olympic Games. This was the first Olympics that allowed women to compete in track and field events. She won a gold and a silver medal in track and came fifth in the 800-metre run—without training for it!

Bobbie helped change the way people felt about women taking part in sports. She did so by excelling in sports, and then through her work as a sportswriter. To honour her, an award was set up in her name. Each year, it is given to Canada's female athlete of the year.

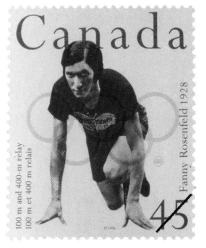

Canada Post issued this stamp in 1996 to honour Bobbie Rosenfeld.

Key Events in the Life of Bobbie Rosenfeld

1904	Born in Russia; family immigrated shortly after to Barrie, Ontario
1923–1933	Took part in many competitions and became known as the world's greatest all around female athlete
1933	Retired from active sports; started a career as a coach and later as a sportswriter
1949	Named to Canada's Sports Hall of Fame at its opening
1950	Chosen as Canada's female athlete of the half-century
1969	Died in Toronto

An Architect with a Unique Design Style

Douglas Cardinal

Can a building reflect the landscape? Can it reflect the spirit of a people? Douglas Cardinal thinks so! Douglas Cardinal is an architect who has developed a distinct design style.

Douglas was born in Calgary, Alberta. His parents were of Siksika (Blackfoot) and Métis heritage. He was interested in architecture from an early age. However, he didn't like the tall, lifeless "glass boxes" so common in cities. He felt that buildings should reflect life and nature.

Douglas studied with great architects and with First Nations Elders. He says they brought out ideas that were always in him.

Douglas Cardinal designed the Canadian Museum of Civilization in Gatineau, Quebec.

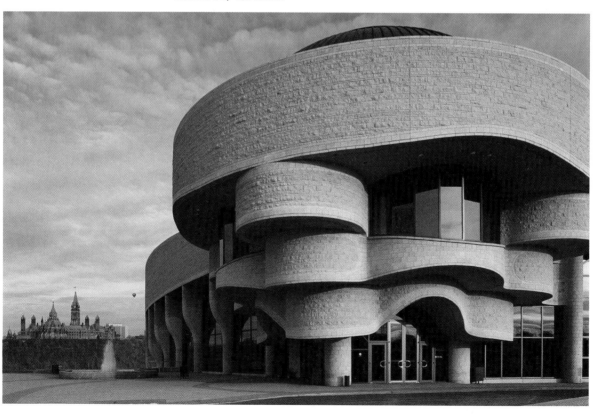

In his building design, Douglas uses curves that blend in with the natural shapes of the land. He uses angles that bring in the sunlight. He often matches the shape of the rooms with the way people will use them.

Many people feel that the Canadian Museum of Civilization and the First Peoples Hall, a permanent exhibit inside the museum, represent Douglas's best work. They say these designs show his sense of vision. Others say, too, that the designs are symbols of Canada. They reflect the past, the present, and the promise of the future.

Douglas Cardinal—Some Architectural Highlights

2004	National Museum of the American Indian, Washington, D.C.
2003	First Nations University of Canada, Saskatchewan
2003	First Peoples Hall in the Canadian Museum of Civilization, Gatineau, Quebec
1989	Canadian Museum of Civilization, Gatineau, Quebec
1976	St. Albert Place, St. Albert, Alberta
1968	St. Mary's Roman Catholic Church, Red Deer, Alberta

A Focus on Unity

Who better to represent Canada's diversity than a woman who came to Canada from Haiti as a young girl? Michaëlle Jean brings a unique perspective to the role of Governor General.

Michaëlle is one of Canada's youngest Governors General. She is also the third woman and the first Black person to hold that office.

◀ Michaëlle Jean meets young Canadians.

Michaëlle Jean

As Governor General, Michaëlle Jean is the Queen's representative in Canada. She travels across the country speaking to Canadians about the value of our many different peoples and what brings them together. She also presents awards, such as the Order of Canada. This award honours outstanding Canadians. At home and overseas, she promotes the beauty, cultures, and arts of Canada.

Here are just a few facts about Michaëlle Jean's life:

- When she was young, her family fled from Haiti and settled in Quebec.
- She speaks five languages.
- She is a respected journalist.
- She was a television and radio show producer and host.
- She has worked with shelters in Quebec and helped hundreds of women and children in crisis.

MEDIA WATCH

Look in newspapers and magazines to find pictures of people who are making a difference in Canada. Explain their importance.

DIG DEEPER

1. What does each person in this selection represent? Why do you think each is seen as a Canadian symbol?

Name	Reason this person is a symbol
Bobbie Rosenfeld	She became an athlete when women were not encouraged...

2. Who has made a difference in your life, school, or community? Write a letter to the person explaining how he or she has made a difference to you.

Captain Canuck:
A Canadian Superhero!

by Edward O'Connor

Canada has its own set of superheroes who have appeared in comic books and comic strips across the country. Perhaps the most famous of these is the incredible Captain Canuck.

What powers might a Canadian superhero have?

Time for a Canadian Superhero

The first Captain Canuck comic book appeared in July 1975. Two young illustrators named Richard Comely and Ron Leishman created the hero. They both grew up reading comic books. They met in Winnipeg in 1971. Soon they discovered they shared the same deep desire. They were tired of reading about American comic book heroes. They thought Canada should have its own superhero.

One day, Leishman drew a picture of a muscular man in a uniform decorated with the maple leaf. Using this design, Comely began to draw storyboards for the comic's first issue. Captain Canuck came to life! The first story was set in the future—1993.

This first Captain Canuck comic book issue from 1975 is now a valuable collector's item.

The Story

It is 1993. Thanks to its natural resources, Canada is the most powerful nation on Earth. Government agent Tom Evans leads a troop of Boy Scouts on a camping trip. Evans wakes up one night to find the boys are missing. Aliens have abducted them!

To try to stop Evans from following them, the aliens zap him with Zeta rays. When Evans comes to, he finds he is twice as strong and twice as fast as any human being on Earth.

The government turns Evans into a symbol of Canadian strength and justice. They give him a costume with Magno boots, a flaring cape, and red and white tights. Captain Canuck will come to the rescue whenever someone threatens the Canadian nation. He will fight against space aliens, political enemies, and criminal gangs.

This was the first chapter of a daily comic strip that was designed to appear in Canadian newspapers.

Captain Canuck's Superhero Profile

Real name: Tom Evans

Regular job: An officer in the Canadian International Security Organization (CISO)

Powers: Super strength, super speed

Costume: Red and white tights, white cowl, heavy gloves, and Magno boots. The Canadian Maple Leaf appears on the front of his cowl and belt buckle.

Allies: CISO agents Kébec (French-Canadian) and Redcoat (an ex-Mountie)

Enemies: Blue Fox, former partner at CISO; financial wizard Mr. Gold; evil genius Nu-Enoch, who uses radioactive sludge to create a race of mutant humans

HE SUDDENLY APPEARED FROM NOWHERE - CLAD IN BRILLIANT CRIMSON AND WHITE; MORE INCREDIBLE, MORE POWERFUL THAN ANY MAN ALIVE! HIS STORY OF BEING HURLED BACK IN TIME, IS MUCH TOO FANTASTIC TO BELIEVE--YET IN THE TURBULENT, TROUBLED TIMES OF 1980 HE IS SO SORELY NEEDED. TO MILLIONS HE'S A CHAMPION FOR JUSTICE--NONETHELESS, WHOEVER OR WHATEVER THEY THINK HIM TO BE -- TOM EVANS KNOWS TOO WELL- HE **IS** AND MUST **REMAIN**...

CAPTAIN CANUCK T.M.

TOMORROW "POWER PLAY"

Captain Canuck Evolves

The first version of Captain Canuck lasted for six years and 14 issues. In the end, the comic became just too expensive to produce. However, Richard Comely and others did not lose interest in the idea. Captain Canuck has appeared several times since 1975—in 1993, 2004, and 2006. His name, career, and sidekicks have often changed to reflect current Canadian issues.

In the 1993 series, he was community leader Darren Oak and one of his most trusted friends was Daniel Blackbird. Blackbird rescued Captain Canuck when he was captured by villains who wanted to control Canada. In the 2006 series, Captain Canuck's new mission was to stop the flow of illegal guns into Canada. Through wars, economic troubles, and internal strife, Captain Canuck has always bounced back!

Captain Canuck trading cards

Captain Canuck™ Legacy Issue #1 Sept/Oct 2006 Published by Comely Comix

This page is from the 2006 issue of Captain Canuck.

In 1995, Canada Post issued a series of stamps honouring Canadian superheroes, including Captain Canuck.

DIG DEEPER

1. Make jot notes telling about a current Canadian issue that Captain Canuck could deal with.

2. Create a story or comic strip that tells how Captain Canuck comes to the rescue. Give him new powers to fit the situation.

What can these stamps tell about Canada?

From: **Canada**

To: **The World**

Canadian Tulip Festival, ON • Festival canadien des tulipes, On

LA SOIRÉE DU HOCKEY

Canada   46

Canada   46

148

CANADA

Agawa Canyon, ON • Canyon Agawa, Ont.

CANADA

Polar Bear Watching • Observation d'ours blancs • MB

CANADA

Peggy's Cove, NS - N.-É.

CANADA 48

Vancouver 2010

VIA AIR
PAR A

R MAIL
VION

IR MA
AVION

DIG DEEPER

1. Choose one of the stamps. What story does it tell? Share your ideas with a group.

2. Create your own stamp to tell a story about your family, school, or community.

Here's our task, Goose: we're going to brand Canada.

Brand Canada?

Branding Canada means coming up with a nifty little phrase or logo that we can use to advertise who we are.

Okay, here's one: "Land of Honking Great Geese!"

Well, certainly wildlife is part of the Canadian appeal. What about something with beavers, Canada's national symbol?

How about: "A Tail-Thwapping Destination!"

Or "A Country You Can Really Chew On!"

What other animal is associated with Canada?

I know, "Canada: A Million Mosquitoes Greet You!"

That's welcoming, but it might make people itchy. Maybe something about Canada's natural wonders. Like: "Discover Our True Nature."

Say, that's good, Moose!

But I didn't make it up. It's used by Canada's tourist industry. We need to come up with something else that captures the idea of our vast wilderness and wide-open spaces.

I've got it, "Canada: We've Got Lots of It!"

Catchy. But what is the "it" that we have lots of?

Bog. We have a lot of bog in Canada.

Hmmmm. Let's take a break and come back to this.

151

152

I have a new idea, Goose. Let's think of pictures or images that say something about Canada. Maybe we could do something along those lines?

I have an idea. How about this?

What about some ideas that don't involve geese? I wondered if we could do something with a canoe? Canoes are very Canadian.

Like this? It shows that Canada is a wild, exciting ride!

Hmmm. Looks a little dangerous, don't you think?

Or better yet, try this. This represents the multicultural nature of Canada—people of many cultural backgrounds all in the same boat.

But everyone looks so squished. Canada is actually very large and welcoming.

I've got it! Try this one.

Why are they paddling in different directions?

Because they're Canadian. They can't agree on where they're going. They're lost in the Canadian wilderness, probably seeking their Canadian identity.

Should we take another break? Then we'll give this branding exercise one more try.

DIG DEEPER

1. What symbols do Moose and Goose use? What other symbols do you think they could have used?

2. Work with a group to complete Moose and Goose's branding exercise. How would your group brand Canada?

153

Celebrations and Ceremonies

by Kelly Cochrane

How do we, in Canada, honour our country, our people, and our heritage?

Canada Day:
The Day We Became a Country

July 1st. It's Canada Day! Across the country, people gather to celebrate Canada's birthday. The colours and symbols of Canadians are everywhere, even on people's faces!

Many people flock to the streets to watch parades. There is music and dancing. Some people gather with friends, family, and neighbours to have backyard barbeques.

How did Canada Day begin? On July 1, 1867, Nova Scotia, New Brunswick, Quebec, and Ontario joined to form a new country. Later, other provinces and territories joined them to form the Canada we know today.

READ LIKE A WRITER

Why doesn't the writer start the first paragraph with a complete sentence?

In Newfoundland and Labrador, July 1st is also known as Memorial Day. This day commemorates the Newfoundlanders who fought and lost their lives during a major battle in World War I.

Remembrance Day:
"Lest We Forget"

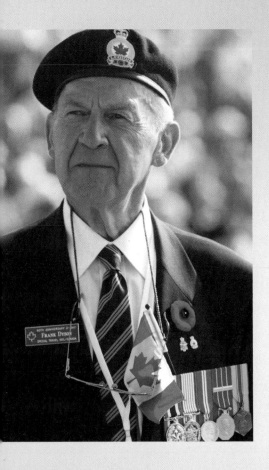

On November 11th, Canadians honour the men and women who fought in wars and participated in peacekeeping duties throughout the world. This tradition began in 1919, after World War I.

On Remembrance Day, communities across the country hold special ceremonies. These often begin with a veterans' march. After the parade, a bugler plays the "Last Post." This is a bugle call to bid goodbye to those who died fighting in war. A two-minute silence follows. Another bugle call, "Reveille," breaks the silence.

In the weeks before, and on November 11th, Canadians wear poppies as a token of remembrance. Poppies grew in the fields of France and Belgium, where many soldiers died in battle during World War I.

National Aboriginal Day:
Celebrating First Peoples

National Aboriginal Day is on June 21st. On this day, Aboriginal peoples celebrate their diverse cultures. They invite Canadians from all walks of life to join in the many events.

It is a day to celebrate with family and friends. Many people take part in both contemporary and traditional dance, song, and other celebrations. They also join in sports and recreational activities.

June 21st was chosen because it is an important day for many Aboriginal cultures. It is the first day of summer and the longest day of the year.

These images show some of the people and events associated with National Aboriginal Day.

Soyez de la fête!   le 21 juin * june 21   Share in the celebration!

Journée nationale des Autochtones

National Aboriginal Day

157

Black History Month

Every year, during Black History Month in February, Canadians are invited to take part in festivities and events that honour the many achievements and contributions of African Canadians, past and present.

One way to participate is through the Mathieu Da Costa Challenge. Mathieu Da Costa is the first recorded person of African heritage to set foot on Canadian soil. The Challenge is a national creative writing and art contest for young people aged 9 to 18. It celebrates the contributions that Canadians of Aboriginal, African, and other backgrounds have made to the building of Canada.

Dragon Boat Races

Dragon boat racing is one of the most important Chinese traditions after Chinese New Year. It is also now a yearly event held in many Canadian communities. According to a Chinese legend, local fishermen saw their well-loved poet, Qu Yuan, jump into the Mei Lo River to protest against the government. They raced out with their boats to save him. Sadly, they arrived too late. Today, people re-enact this scene to save Qu Yuan by taking part in the popular dragon boat race. Combine the race with food, entertainment, community spirit, and charitable fundraising, and you have a festival!

DIG DEEPER

1. Why is it important for people to celebrate special days? Share your ideas with a partner.

2. What other special days do Canadians celebrate? Write a poem to describe or create a poster to illustrate one celebration.

Canadians have other opportunities to get together throughout the year for some rather unusual events.

In South River, ON, people join in the annual Black Fly Hunt every spring!

Every year, some Canadians in Vancouver, BC, welcome the new year by joining in the Polar Bear Swim at English Bay!

Dramatists at Work!

It's your turn to tell others about celebrations and special events. Form a small group and share through drama.

What Will Your Drama Be About?

- Choose a celebration or special event that interests you.
- Decide where you will perform and for whom.
- Make a list or a web with main ideas and details.
- Choose the most important information you want your audience to learn.

IDEAS TO TRY

- Get advice from someone who knows about drama.
- Make a list of characters and jobs.
- Sketch what a scene might look like.

Create and Polish Your Script

- Plan what will take place.
- Create a script—include directions telling characters how to speak and act.
- Consider adding props or appropriate clothing.
- Work as a team to check and polish your script.

Practise, Practise, Practise

- Find time to practise.
- Make sure you learn your parts!
- Practise your actions as well as your words.
- Help one another improve.
- Make improvements until the final practice.

THINGS TO REMEMBER

- Create the right mood.
- The purpose is to provide information—a narrator might help with this.

Performers, Please!

- Share your performance with an audience.

Ways to Share

- Perform for your class or invited guests.
- Involve your audience by asking them what they learned.
- Videotape your presentation.

How can a quilt be a symbol of Canada?

162

Quilt of Belonging

by Janice Weaver

Esther Bryan is a visual artist. She has always believed that Canada is a richer country because of what people have brought, and continue to bring, to it. After a trip to her father's homeland of Slovakia, her belief was even stronger. She began to think more about the world and her place in it. Esther realized that, although each of us experiences life in our own unique way, we also have much in common. She became convinced that every single person in the world—regardless of age, abilities, or circumstances of life—has something of value to offer, a contribution to make.

READ LIKE A WRITER

How does the author join ideas in sentences?

Métis

China

When Esther came back to Canada, she began to think about ways to honour the contributions of all peoples. "I wanted to create something that would celebrate the whole fabric that is Canada," she says.

She decided to make a huge quilt. It would be a monument in stitches and fabric. It would honour the "patchwork" of people who came to Canada from many places and helped build the country. The quilt would include a block for every nation of the world and for all the Aboriginal nations living in Canada. Each block would be prepared by someone in Canada with a connection to that nation or group.

In the end, the Quilt of Belonging has become a powerful symbol of Canada. All the blocks are separate and unique, like the people who created them and the nations they represent. Each one is also connected to its neighbours by a continuous length of thread. This is a colourful strand that links the blocks just as we are linked to our fellow citizens by our obligations and responsibilities as Canadians.

"The quilt is a vision of what we can and should be," Esther says. "There can be a place for everyone in Canada and in the world, just as there is a place for everyone in the Quilt of Belonging."

Egypt

India

DIG DEEPER

1. Choose a quilt block from the selection. Identify symbols you see and tell how you think they represent the people or nation. Research any symbols you do not recognize.

2. Create a paper quilt block design to represent your family or community. Join yours with those of classmates or friends to make a large paper quilt.

Heroes of
Isle aux Morts

by Alice Walsh • Illustrations by Geoff Butler

What symbols can you identify in this story?

Anne Harvey was a Newfoundland girl, born to the sea. For as long as she could remember, she had fished with her father along the rugged shores of Isle aux Morts. She loved the great sea, but she feared it too. There were dangerous reefs and shoals, and no lighthouses to guide the tiny fishing boats. Many fishermen went to sea, never to return.

READ LIKE A WRITER

How is the characters' dialogue different from other sentences in the story?

Ships of every description passed by the island's massive cliffs. Sometimes Anne found silk handkerchiefs, fine linen, and pieces of china that had been washed up with the tide. They came from ships that had never reached their destination—ships that had sunk or had run aground.

Early one morning in July 1832, Anne awoke to a raging storm. Wind rattled the stovepipes and shook the glass in the windows. The great sea rose and fell. Waves rushed up to shore and thundered against the cliffs. The little fishing boats, tied to their moorings, tossed and rolled wildly.

We won't be going fishing this morning, Anne told herself. Suddenly she heard a distress signal. Then another, and another. A flare lit up the dark sky, and she knew a ship was in trouble.

Quickly she dressed and ran to the lookout at the top of the hill.

In the grey morning light, she could barely make out the ghostly shape of a ship that had been driven upon a rock. Waves smashed against the ship's side. Anne knew that if help did not arrive soon, the ship would be smashed to pieces by the savage waves.

Anne wasted no time running back to the house. Her father was still asleep, but she shook him awake. "Papa, get up," she said. "A ship has run aground."

George Harvey bolted up. "Another one?"

He had seen many shipwrecks and knew of many lives lost. In fact, that was how the island got its name. Isle aux Morts means Island of the Dead.

gaff
a stick with an iron hook

dory
a small flat-bottom fishing boat

forecastle
the forward part of a ship

"Go wake Thomas," he said.

While Anne went to wake her young brother, her father put on oilskins and rubber boots. He gathered rope, a gaff, and a knife. In no time, they were all on the beach, ready to launch the dory. Hairy Man, their dog, followed them to the wharf and, when they got into the boat, he jumped in with them.

Anne took one oar and her father took the other. Together they struggled against the fierce gale. Waves broke under the boat, nearly capsizing it. At times they curled over the bow, sending showers of sea spray down upon them. While Anne and her father rowed, Thomas bailed out the water with a tin can.

As they neared the ship, they could see the word *Despatch* on her bow. They could hear the moans and cries of the frightened passengers who crowded the forecastle—the only part of the ship that was out of reach of the pounding waves. The fierce wind and rough sea kept the dory from getting close enough to help.

"We must find a way to get a rope to them," George Harvey said, anxiously. Mountainous waves crashed on the *Despatch*'s deck. She was starting to go to pieces. Her lifeboats were smashed. Broken paddles and bits of wood floated around in the water.

"We could send Hairy Man," Anne suggested. "You knows what a good swimmer *he* is."

Her father nodded slowly, remembering the times Hairy Man braved the rough waters to fetch ducks, geese, and other seabirds he had shot. But from the frown that deepened her father's brow, Anne knew he held little hope for the passengers of the *Despatch*.

"Go, Hairy Man! Go, b'y," Anne pointed him in the direction of the ship.

Obediently, the dog jumped into the water and was immediately swallowed by a giant wave. Anne waited anxiously until his head rose above the churning sea. As he swam toward the doomed ship, enormous waves buried him again and again. Each time, Anne held her breath until he resurfaced.

Among the passengers who huddled in the forecastle were gentlemen and grand ladies, their ruffled shirts and silk dresses ruined from the salt sea. There were men in britches and children in rags, all of them watching fearfully as the dog struggled against the violent sea.

Hairy Man did not stop swimming until he reached the *Despatch*. As eager hands lifted him aboard, a cheer went up from the crowd. A rope was tied around his middle and he was instructed to go back to his master's boat. As the dog again faced the dangerous waves, the line was carefully let out behind him.

breeches buoy

a pair of short pants fastened to a belt or life preserver used in rescue operations at sea

Anne and her father rowed to shore with the rope Hairy Man had brought them. George Harvey fastened it to a pole in the ground, enabling the crew to make a breeches buoy.

Grasping the rope, one hundred and sixty-three passengers made their way, one by one, over the dangerous sea to the shores of Isle aux Morts.

The *Despatch* had come from England, on her way to Quebec. English, Newfoundland, and French voices now filled the air. Hairy Man, the centre of attention, ran and hid behind the stove.

The unexpected guests stayed on the island for over a week, and all the families on Isle aux Morts shared their flour, fish, molasses, and tea. At night, in houses all over the island,

the guests slept in featherbeds, on daybeds, and even on floors.

One day the supply ship came, and took the visitors away.

"Thank you for having us on your island," a gentleman said, rather formally.

"Good of yous to drop by," said George Harvey, winking at Anne.

"Good-bye."

"*Au revoir.*"

"Cheerio."

And then they were gone.

But the Harveys were not forgotten. Everywhere the passengers went, they told of their rescue by a courageous Newfoundland family and their dog. In St. John's, in Canada, and even in England, people heard of the Harveys' brave deed. Eventually, the news reached the king of England. He was so impressed by the tale that he sent them one hundred gold sovereigns. He even had a special gold medal struck for presentation, with an inscription telling of the family's bravery.

There was a personal letter for each of them, praising them for their deeds. The letter was signed by good King George: "To the heroes of Isle aux Morts."

DIG DEEPER

1. What qualities did Hairy Man exhibit that made him a hero? Give examples from the story.

2. Choose a dramatic part of the story and write it as a play. Remember to use descriptive words in the instructions to the characters. Describe how the characters are to speak or act.

The Song Within My Heart

by David Bouchard • Paintings by Allen Sapp

How can songs, dances, and stories make you feel you belong?

Listen to the beating drum
It tells a hundred stories
Of our people, of our homeland
Some of birds and beasts and sweet grass.

Close your eyes and listen
You might come to hear a story
That no one hears but you alone
A story of your very own.

READ LIKE A WRITER
How does the author make
you feel a beat or a
rhythm in this poem?

BOOM boom boom boom BOOM boom boom boom
    BOOM boom boom boom BOOM boom boom boom.
   BOOM boom boom boom BOOM boom boom boom
    BOOM boom boom boom BOOM boom boom boom.

Listen to the singers
They are also telling stories
Some of pleasure, some of sorrow
Some of birth or life here after.

Close your eyes and listen
You might come to hear a story
That no one hears but you alone
Another of your very own.

HEY hey hey hey Hi hey hey hey
   HI hey hey hey HEY hey hi.
    HEY hey hey hey Hi hey hey hey
     HI hey hey hey HEY hey hey!

When at first I heard them
I was standing near my Nokum
I stood staring at my elder
Who was lost somewhere in deepest thought.

When at first I heard them
I was standing with my Nokum
Who smiled and began swaying
Closed her eyes and started singing.
Not loud at first, a simple hum
I tugged with force on both her arms.

"Grandma," I called out to her
"I don't know what they're saying!"
She couldn't or she didn't hear
Yet I was loud and she was near.

"Grandma," I yelled out again
"Please tell me what they're saying."
She smiled as she looked down at me
And taught me how to hear and see.

HEY hey hey hey Hi hey hey hey

HI hey hey hey HEY hey hi.

HEY hey hey hey Hi hey hey hey

HI hey hey hey HEY hey hey!

"Child," she said, "There are some things
That you can call your very own.
Not toys or clothes, not jewels or cars
Don't ever make these things your own."

"There aren't a lot but there *are* things
That you should learn to call your own.
Your stories, songs and beating heart
Are truly yours and yours alone."

HEY hey hey hey Hi hey hey hey

      HI hey hey hey HEY hey hi.

            HEY hey hey hey Hi hey hey hey

                  HI hey hey hey HEY hey hey!

And right there at that pow-wow
(Nokum knew the time for teaching)
The scorching sun echoed the drums
The dancers would be soon to come.

"Yes child," she said, "There are some things
That you can call your very own.
Your stories, songs and beating heart
Are truly yours and yours alone."

HEY hey hey hey Hi hey hey hey

HI hey hey hey HEY hey hi.

HEY hey hey hey Hi hey hey hey

HI hey hey hey HEY hey hey!

HEY hey hey hey Hi hey hey hey

HI hey hey hey HEY hey hi.

HEY hey hey hey Hi hey hey hey

HI hey hey hey HEY hey hey!

"A story is a sacred thing
That should be passed from age to youth
I choose to share my best with you
That you might own and share them too."

"And never use another's tale
Unless he knows and he approves.
And only then and then alone
Might you tell it to others."

HEY hey hey hey Hi hey hey hey

HI hey hey hey HEY hey hi.

HEY hey hey hey Hi hey hey hey

HI hey hey hey HEY hey hey!

"And much the same, the beating drum
It echoes that which is your soul
You seek a rhythm that is true
Of all the secrets that are you."

"So much of what the drummer feels
Is clear with every beat you hear.
He bares it all, he cannot hide.
He's sharing what he is inside."

BOOM boom boom boom BOOM boom boom boom

BOOM boom boom boom BOOM boom boom.

BOOM boom boom boom BOOM boom boom boom

BOOM boom boom boom BOOM boom boom.

"And of the things in my own life
That I have owned, there are none so dear
As songs I sing and stories tell
All tales that you should know by now."

"To understand the song I sing
Close your eyes and listen
And try to hear the subtle things
It is your Nokum's heart that sings."

HEY hey hey hey Hi hey hey hey

HI hey hey hey HEY hey hi.

HEY hey hey hey Hi hey hey hey

HI hey hey hey HEY hey hey!

If you, dear reader, hear me sing
And can't make out my message
You should not fret, I was like you
I had to learn to listen too!

To understand the song I sing
Close your eyes and listen
And try to hear the subtle things
It's of my Nokum that I sing.

HEY hey hey hey Hi hey hey hey

HI hey hey hey HEY hey hi.

HEY hey hey hey Hi hey hey hey

HI hey hey hey HEY hey hey!

Allen Sapp is a Wood Cree artist from Saskatchewan. The picture at right is his grandmother (Nokum). David Bouchard's poem is about a young boy going to his first pow-wow with his Nokum.

Nokum

Allen Sapp

DIG DEEPER

1. Practise reading the poem aloud in a group. Each group member could read different parts of the poem.

2. Reread the words of the grandmother and look at the paintings. How would you describe the relationship between the boy and his grandmother?

Connect and Share

You've learned about people and symbols of Canada.
It's your turn to have fun with the information!
Work with a group to make a television game show.

Share information!

- Choose a favourite topic from this unit.
- Tell someone at home about it.
- Ask for ideas for your game show.

Create a game show!

- Each group member makes five question cards with answers on the back.
- Decide on rules for the game, props for the show, and roles for group members.
- Invite players to take part in your show. Have fun!

Spotlight on Learning

Collect

- Gather your notebooks, writing, and projects from this unit.

Talk and reflect

Work with a partner.

- Together, read the Learning Goals on page 122.
- Talk about how well you met these goals.
- Look through your work for evidence.

Select

- Choose two pieces of work that show how you achieved the Learning Goals. (The same piece of work can show more than one goal.)

Tell about your choices

- Tell what each piece shows about your learning.

My choices	I want this in my portfolio because...

Reflect

- What have you learned about gathering and presenting information on social studies topics?
- What have you discovered about people and symbols of Canada?

Acknowledgements

Permission to reprint copyrighted material is gratefully acknowledged. Every effort has been made to trace ownership of all copyrighted material and to secure permission from copyright holders. In the event of any questions arising as to the use of any material, we will be pleased to make the necessary corrections in future printings.

Student Book

Photographs

2–3 Thomas Barwick/Photodisc/Getty Images; **8 t** kayakmag.ca © Canada's National History Society 2006, **l** www.cbc.ca/kids © cbc.ca, **middle** Toronto Star, **r** www.nwsd.ca/schools/gateway/broadcasts.htm used with permission of Gateway Elementary School; **9** Ray Boudreau; **10** John Maschak; **11** John Maschak; **12** Courtesy of the Molgat Family; **13** Courtesy of the Molgat Family; **iv, 14** Amanjeet Chauhan; **15** Amanjeet Chauhan; **16 t** Ray Boudreau, **b** Ciaran Griffin/Stockbyte/Getty Images; **17** Ray Boudreau; **18** Courtesy of Right To Play, www.righttoplay.ca; **19** UPI Photo/Gary C. Caskey/Landov; **20** Courtesy of Right To Play; **21 t** CP/Paul Chiasson, **b** Courtesy of Right To Play; **22** CP/Abaca/Steve Deslich; **23 t** © Adams Picture Library t/a apl/Alamy, **b and v** © Nikolay Okhitin/Shutterstock; **24** © Royalty-Free/Corbis; **25** NRCan Topographic Maps, Lake Lavieille, Nipissing District, Ontario Series A751, 31 E/16, Edition 5, © 2007. Produced under licence from Her Majesty the Queen in Right of Canada, with permission of Natural Resources Canada; **26** Jeff Coates, Indianapolis, IN. www.truenorth360.com. Used with permission; **27 l** © OkapiStudio/Shutterstock, **middle** Shutterstock, **r** © PhotoObjects/Jupiterimages, **b** CP/AP Photo/Paul Sakuma; **28 tl** Pearson Image Library, **tr and middle** © PhotoObjects/Jupiterimages, **b** CP/Hamilton Spectator/Cathie Coward; **29 t** Reuters/David Loh/Landov, **middle l** © PhotoObjects/Jupiterimages, **middle r** © Comstock/Jupiterimages, **b** Reuters/HO/Landov; **v, 30 t** AP Wide World Photos, **middle** CP/AP Photo/Bob Child, **b** © ajt/Shutterstock; **36–39 background** Shutterstock; **36 tl** Shutterstock, **tr** Used with permission of BC Breakers, **bl** Used with permission of Kawartha Lakes Minor Lacrosse Association, **br** Used with permission of the Swift River Broncos Hockey Club, **background** Shutterstock; **37 tl** Courtesy of the Saint John Sea Dogs Hockey Club, **tr** Courtesy of Six Nations Arrows Express Jr. A Lacrosse Team, **middle** Courtesy of Montreal Alouettes Football Club, **bl** Courtesy of NAIT Athletics, **br** Courtesy of the Paralympic Sports Association, **background** Shutterstock; **38 tl** Used with permission of the Vancouver Giants, **tr** Used with permission of Seneca College Department of Athletics and Recreation, **bl** Used with permission of the London Knights Hockey Inc. of the Ontario Hockey League, **br** Used with permission of Brandon University Athletics Department, Manitoba **background** Shutterstock; **39 l** Used with permission of Rugby Canada, **r** Used with permission of Canada Basketball, www.basketball.ca; **background tr and b** Shutterstock; **40–41** Ray Boudreau; **42** © Stockdisc/Getty Images; **43** Courtesy of the HOPE Initiative; **44** © 2004 Lucasfilm Entertainment Company Ltd., Courtesy of the Greater Bay Area Make-A-Wish Foundation®, www.makewish.org; **45 (all)** Courtesy of the HOPE Initiative; **46–47** FOXTROT © 2002 Bill Amend. Reprinted with permission of UNIVERSAL PRESS SYNDICATE. All rights reserved, **background** © GOODSHOOT/Jupiterimages; **60** Ray Boudreau; **61** © Asia Images Group/AsiaPix/Getty Images; **62–63** © Imagestate/First Light; **64–67 background** © AbleStock/Jupiterimages; **64** © Mary Evans Picture Library/Alamy; **65** © Mary Evans Picture Library/Alamy; **66** © Horace Bristol/Corbis; **67** Stephen Frink/Image Bank/Getty Images; **68 t** www.kids-mysteries.com used with permission, **b l–r** © Pictorial Press Ltd./Alamy, Cover of THE GREAT ADVENTURES OF SHERLOCK HOLMES by Arthur Conan Doyle (Puffin, 1994). Reproduced by permission of Penguin Books Ltd., From *Monster in the Mountains* by Shane Peacock. Copyright © Shane Peacock, 2003. Cover illustrated by Brian Deines and designed by Martin Gould. Reprinted by permission of the illustrator and Penguin Group (Canada), a Division of Pearson Canada Inc.; **69** Ray Boudreau; **76 t** Ray Boudreau, **b** Comstock/ Jupiterimages; **77** Ray Boudreau; **94–95** Ray Boudreau; **95** Anne MacInnes; **98** CP/Robert Dall; **99** Heath Moffatt Photography. Used by permission of Eric Wilson, www.ericwilson.com; **100** *The Inuk Mountie Adventure*. Copyright © 1995 by Eric Hamilton Wilson. Cover and chapter illustrations copyright © 1995 by Richard Row. Published by HarperCollins Publishers Ltd. All rights reserved, *Red River Ransom*. Copyright © 2006 by Eric Wilson Enterprises, Inc. Cover and chapter illustrations by Derek Mah. Published by HarperCollins Publishers Ltd. All rights reserved, *Code Red at the Supermall*. Text © 1988 by Eric Hamilton Wilson. Copyright renewed 2003 by Eric Wilson Enterprises, Inc. Cover and chapter illustrations by Richard Row. Published by HarperCollins Publishers Ltd. All rights reserved; **120** Ray Boudreau; **121** Comstock/Jupiterimages; **viii, 124–125** coin images © courtesy of the Royal Canadian Mint/Image des pièces © courtoisie de la Monnaie royale canadienne; **124** © Stock Connection Distribution/ Alamy; **125** © blickwinkel/Alamy, **126** coin images © courtesy of the Royal Canadian Mint/Image des pièces © courtoisie de la Monnaie royale canadienne, **t** CP PHOTO/Andrew Vaughan, **b** Jupiterimages Unlimited; **127 t** Darcy Philips. Used with permission of Michael Mitchell & MKM Music Productions Ltd, **m** Destrubé Photo. Used with permission of Michael Mitchell & MKM Music Productions Ltd., **b** B&C Alexander/FirstLight; **128 t** Courtesy of World Life Video Productions, Toronto. Www.ontopoftheworld.ca, **bl** Mercury Graphics. Used with permission of Michael Mitchell & MKM Music Productions Ltd., **m** The Symbols of Canada (http://www.pch.gc.ca/progs/cpsc-ccsp/sc-cs/ index_e.cfm). The Department of Canadian Heritage. Reproduced with the permission of the Minister of Public Works and Government Services Canada, 2006, **r** Taken from The RCMP Musical Ride © 2004 text and illustrations by Maxwell Newhouse, published in Canada by Tundra Books, Toronto; **viii, 130** AP Photo/Kevork Djansezian; **131** Photo courtesy of the Department of Canadian Heritage. Reproduced with the permission of the Minister of Public Works and Government Services of Canada, 2007; **132** Jerry Kobalenko/Firstlight, **inset** Courtesy of the Nunavut Legislative Assembly; **133 t** CP PHOTO/Jonathan Hayward, **b** © David Fleetham/Alamy; **134** CP PHOTO/Ottawa Citizen-Chris Mikula; **135 t** © Robert Harding Picture Library Ltd./Alamy, **b** Reprinted with the permission of the RCMP; **136 t** Ray Boudreau, **b** © Picture Partners/maXximages.com; **137** Ray Boudreau; **138** CP PHOTO 1999 (National Archives of Canada) PA-151007; **139** © Canada Post Corporation. Reproduced with permission; **140 t** Photo by Malak, Ottawa, **b** © Ron Watts/CORBIS; **141** CP PHOTO/ Marianne Helm; **142** Photography by Sgt Éric Jolin; **148–149 background** PhotoObjects/ Jupiterimages; **148 t** © Canada Post Corporation 2000. Reproduced with permission, **l** © Canada Post Corporation. Reproduced with permission, **m** © Canada Post Corporation 1999. Reproduced with permission, **r** © Canada Post Corporation 1999. Reproduced with permission; **149 tl** © Canada Post Corporation 2002. Reproduced with permission, **tr** © Canada Post Corporation 2003. Reproduced with permission, **bl** © Canada Post Corporation 2002. Reproduced with permission, **br** © Canada Post Corporation 2002. Reproduced with permission; **154** Benjamin Rondel/Firstlight; **155** Firstlight; **156 t** Getty Images, **b** © Richard Cummins/CORBIS; **157 l** Canadian Press, **r** National Aboriginal Day Calendar 2004-2005. Indian and Northern Affairs Canada, 2005. Reproduced with the permission of the Minister of Public Works and Government Services, 2007; **158** Courtesy of Toronto Chinese Business Association; **159** The Mathieu Da Costa Challenge, The Department of Canadian Heritage. Reproduced with the permission of the Minister of Public Works and Government Services Canada, 2006; **160** Ray Boudreau; **161 t** Ray Boudreau, **b** © Paul Rapson/Alamy; **ix, 162–165** Ken McLaren. By permission of Quilt of Belonging; **180** Ray Boudreau; **181** Comstock/Jupiterimages

Illustrations

iv, 4–7 Ramón Pérez; **32** Dave Whamond; **33–35** Ramón Pérez; **46–47** © Bill Amend; **v, 48, 50–51** Stephen T. Johnson; **v, 52–59** © Kat Thacker; **vi, 64** Steve MacEachern; **vi, 70–75** Leanne Franson; **vii, 78–81** Max Licht; **vii, 82–87** Peter Lacalamita; **vii, 101–103** Luc Melansonn; **vii, 104–111** © Roger Roth; **vii, 112–119** © Martin Springett; **ix, 143–147** CAPTAIN CANUCK registered trademark and copyright owned by Richard D. Comely. All rights reserved; **ix, 150–153**

Solution to "The Case of the Sneak Thief's Sneakers" on pages 78–81
Mona did it. She was the only one of the three people with SkyMaster sneakers who was tall enough to reach the shelf *and* had arms too thick to reach the last dollar.

Posters
Photographs

Illustrations